Praise for *Great Big YES!*

"If you want to be inspired and filled with God's Grace, read this gorgeous compilation of Sue's soul pouring out onto the pages. Her honesty, faith and humor will make you feel uplifted, seen, inspired and closer to God. An absolute gorgeous journey."

—Davis Ehrler
Author of *Kate* and *Do You Remember?*

"Ever since we met, I've known of this book. The Lord has been creating this book since the day Sue was born and what has been created is Holy. It is the voice of the Lord and His expression in Sue's words and life musings. You will relate and find authenticity in every story! It's sitting on a cozy couch over coffee with your dearest friend. It's laying in the lap of your softest elder, it's being cheered for by your biggest fan! Settle in and allow yourself to be known, validated, understood and guided through Sue's wise and honest life lessons. You will begin to make a list of all who need to read this book and it will be a long list!"

—Amy Hoyte
Founder of Beautifully Made Adventures

"Sue's stories are written with humor, wit, and good old fashioned honesty! I love how relatable her writing is. I left each story swept up in the goodness of our overcoming spirit. The way she helps to draw out our testimony while holding space for our humanity, is unparalleled."

—Jonnie Goodmanson
Founder of Live Free Trainings

"This book encompasses so much of what makes us heal and grow. First, a glimpse into her personal stories brings us to the great revelation of not being alone; we find more of ourselves through her vulnerability. Second, her stories allow us to consider how and where God is found in our everyday lives. This book is playful and clever, and also inviting and exposing. Sue delivers a deep sense of wrestling and wondering as God has found her in the very midst of her journey and her willingness to lay it down onto the paper is a testimony and tribute to how very important our lives and stories are to the God who created us. This book invites us to be truly seen and known; to ask questions that have probably haunted us but now feel like an intentional treasure hunt for our souls to feel their worth!"

—Sarah Hall
Experiential Therapist and Founder of Salt and Spirit

"In *Great Big YES! Stories of God's Grace*, Sue shares fun and relatable stories of her life experiences and how God met her with grace each time! The stories pull you in and remind you of a time you walked through the same experience, but Sue takes that story and asks meaningful questions to help you see from a different perspective. Sometimes we need to see our stories differently and ask God, 'What do you want me to learn from this?' Sue reminds us just how gracious God is with us!"

—Tara Royer Steele
Author, Speaker and Gatherer

This book is dedicated to my Mom.
She has been my biggest cheerleader from
day one. Her inexhaustible enthusiasm,
deep abiding faith and love of books
have all rubbed off on me. I'm so grateful.
Thanks for making life so much fun Mom!

Printed in the United States of America
First Edition 2023

Scripture quotations marked (NIV) are taken from the HOLY BIBLE, NEW INTERNATIONAL VERSION®. NIV®. Copyright © 1973, 1978, 1984 by International Bible Society. Used by permission of Zondervan. All rights reserved worldwide.

Scripture quotations marked (ESV) are from The ESV® Bible (The Holy Bible, English Standard Version®), copyright © 2001 by Crossway, a publishing ministry of Good News Publishers. Used by permission. All rights reserved.

Scripture quotations marked (NLT) are from Holy Bible, New Living Translation, copyright © 1996, 2004, 2015 by Tyndale House Foundation. All rights reserved. Used by permission of Tyndale House Publishers, Carol Stream, Illinois 60188.

Scripture quotations marked (MSG) are from THE MESSAGE. Copyright © by Eugene H. Peterson 1993, 2002, 2005, 2018. Used by permission of NavPress. All rights reserved. Represented by Tyndale House Publishers.

ISBN (paperback): 979-8-85460-355-3
ISBN (hardcover): 979-8-85458-324-4

Editing: melanieschitwood.com
Author photo: jennalesterphotography.com
Book cover design and interior formatting: Nelly Murariu, PixBeeDesign.com

Great Big YES!

Stories of God's Grace

SUE BIDSTRUP

He works on us in all sorts of ways; not only through what we think our "religious life." He works through Nature, through our own bodies, through books—sometimes through experiences which seem (at the time) anti-Christian. But above all, He works on us through each other.

—C.S. Lewis, *Mere Christianity*

CONTENTS

We Live and Learn

Some of us are old enough to finally have what they call "perspective." Who knows, though? I don't want to be cocky. Maybe I should be as embarrassed by whatever "wisdom" I'm spouting now as I am of how I once thought it important to discuss the benefits of an "academic preschool."

Actually, I didn't do that. I was too busy feigning nonchalance. Only uptight moms worried about this nonsense. I'm enlightened and not competitive. I will embrace my child's own unique pace. *Wait, is that preschool better? Will she be behind? What time do we need to get in line? Letters of recommendation???*

You know how it is. We were all better mothers before we were mothers. Or before we started comparing. Or before our kids turned out to be real-live, individual humans with unique needs.

Now I know better. Which is to say I know I don't know. Which is good because the scariest place to be is clueless without a clue that you're clueless. Aka to be young again.

So we older ladies have earned the right to state things as if they are fact. At just the same time we realize we have no facts. The ever-changing reality is, well, ever-changing.

Writing is my happy place. It has always helped me process. It's the theme that runs consistently throughout my life—reading and writing. I started a blog in 2010 called, *Great Big YES*. I wanted to write about God and faith and motherhood and life. I didn't have a master plan for my future, but I did always dream of writing a book. So to say that I'm excited you are holding this book is an understatement. I'm thrilled!

It took time to get here. Over the last thirteen years, my desire to publish my writing waxed and waned. But I kept writing because it helped me so much personally. Writing feels like a big exhale, a break, a moment to myself to go inside and think and organize my thoughts. As I was putting together the essays for this book, I went through everything I've written since 2010. What a gift it is to be able to have stories and thoughts from the past saved in writing! I've gathered my favorites and included them here.

I love encouraging other people to write too. As a life coach, I know that journal writing is an amazing tool for discovery and processing. When we write our stories, our thoughts, and our experiences, we can look at the whole picture with fresh eyes and recognize the divine threads and holy moments of our lives. This helps us to have gratitude and face the future with joyful expectation!

Journaling helps us process what is going on in our hearts and minds. Through the practice of writing, we can find mental, emotional, and spiritual release and healing. Journaling allows us to create space between our negative thoughts. It gives us time to take every thought captive and ask, *Is this true? Is this what God would say? Is this helpful?* And then ultimately, *How else can I look at this? How do I approach this with the eyes of faith? Where is God leading me?*

As I was putting this book together, I didn't want it to be all about me and my stories. I provide them as jumping-off points.

My goal is that you will feel inspired to write your own stories. To that end, I've included journal prompts at the end of each essay. To anyone who knows me, they will not be surprised by the fact that I'm providing questions. I am the dinner party guest who always comes ready with questions for the table, and I have spent many late nights as the fire pit conversation starter.

We are all on a personal journey, both emotionally and spiritually. At some point in our life, we have to say *yes* to God's invitation to live our lives, embrace our gifts and our challenges, leave our comfort zones, slay our dragons, and become who we were created to be. Just like I have my stories, you have yours. When we write them out and take a look at them, we realize that transformation has taken place in our hearts and minds. Over time, we have had fears and doubts, we have battled, and we have grown. We have been made new. Our trust in God is renewed.

I'm not sure why you bought this book. Be honest, did my mom give it to you as a gift? I wouldn't doubt that she bought them all up and is handing them out at a church gathering while serving a casserole right now. She is always and has always been my biggest fan. I wouldn't even know how to love books if it wasn't for her. From the time I was a baby, she had me at library storytime. She was a reading teacher and she and my dad owned a bookstore when I was growing up, so I inherited this love of stories.

While I can't offer answers or "to-dos" to help you avoid any pitfalls or pain, my prayer is to offer you something better. Hope. Laughter. Recognition. Encouragement. Permission. I hope you feel comforted. Less alone. Since I'm human and messy and multifaceted, like you are, some essays might feel like a cozy blanket, a cup of tea, and time getting centered. (Wait, scratch that. I don't drink tea. I mean a cup of *strong* coffee.) Other times, I hope you feel like your best friend just entered the room like a whirlwind with unwashed hair and lots of sass, feverishly dishing out her latest escapade.

We need that, don't we? We spend a lot of time (Okay, me. I spend a lot of time) trying to be the former, the wise and calm one. And I seek that out too. We all need that. But what we all also need every once in a while is to have the messy friend come over and verbally vomit on us. *Tell me everything,* we say as we settle in to listen. If we want to have that friend, we have to be that friend. Here goes!

I'm so grateful for all of it.

FOUNDATIONS OF GRACE

Lord, thanks for the memories. As we write about our childhood and our parents and siblings and the foundation that was built in our early lives, in our family of origin, please be with us. Some memories sting and others make us feel good, but You are in it all.

*I remember You in the light that came through my bedroom window. I was young and bored, just daydreaming. I was on my canopy bed with a ruffled comforter, my walls covered with Shaun Cassidy posters. The **Grease** soundtrack was playing, and the light was shining through.*

I lay there, just staring into space. And in the light, there were these little fly-away things, little dots, dust probably, but I picture that was You, saying "Hi." Showing up. Sparkling.

So much of our growth is waiting. So much of our learning is uncomfortable and unknown. But You are not either of those things. There is a quietness to You. Sure, You can roar like thunder, but when I think of my childhood, it's in the quiet that I remember feeling peace. I believe that was You. Prickles of light. Whispers of love. Always available when my eyes were open to notice.

God, You are our true foundation. You are our family of origin. You are our Father. When we understand that, our identity is secure. We are worthy and beloved. Help us believe it. Show us Your grace in our stories. Help us see Your sovereign hand in our unique journey. Remind us that wherever we came from, it's all holy ground.

Thank you, Lord, for the people who have loved us. Thank you for the laughs and the tears and the "aha" moments. Thanks for all of it. We trust none of it is wasted.

Amen. Amen. Yes and Amen.

It All Starts with a Note

"I am running away." This is what I wrote in a note to my parents when I was eight years old. It continued, "I will leave at seven."

My dad found the note. Then he carried it in his wallet for years. It illustrated me perfectly.

A responsible rebel.

A wanna-be wild child packaged in a rule-follower.

A dreamer, dedicated to doing the right thing.

My eight-year-old self was looking for confirmation that her parents didn't want her to go. Just to be sure, I spilled the beans and then begged for rescue. I still remember I packed my sleeping bag, pink with orange and white flowers. I rolled it into its matching bag and shoved some other stuff in there. God only knows what I grabbed. I know for sure I brought my journal. I've always kept one. You know, to record all the wild and crazy adventures of my life.

Turns out, my life isn't wild and crazy. But it is an adventure. And I'm still carrying a journal around, writing about it.

While my younger self may have thought the good stuff would be found in running, I know now that the best stories, the juiciest relationships, and the deepest wisdom we seek come from staying. Anyone can run. It takes a hero to stay.

My dad was waiting for me that morning on the steps. He got there before seven. I knew he would. But I tested him anyway. He was one of the good ones. Steadfast. Kind. Wise. Dependable. He loved me well. He was a stayer. My own personal hero.

Having a dad like mine prepared me for God's love. God, my other Father, who I run from and write notes to and continue to test. Who also is the recipient of me spilling the beans and begging for rescue. He shows up too. Every time. Early, waiting, prepared to hear why I want to leave, ready to love me into staying.

I'm so grateful to my mom and dad and my heavenly Father because they stayed. And they taught me how to stay too. They taught me the importance of rooting down. They taught me to own my identity as beloved and cherished. That's where our power lies. It's not out there somewhere. It's at home. With God. It's with our people in the place where we are. Today. Now.

It all started with a note. And a journal. Because our words matter, and they allow us to share our stories. Our stories bring clarity and purpose. Our life, as we are living it, is an adventure. We just need to open our eyes and look around. Wherever we are, we are standing on holy ground. Let's write about it.

* What is something that happened in your childhood that had a lasting effect on you?

* Do you consider yourself a rule-follower, a rebel, or a mixture of both?

* When in your life has God asked you to stay?

Honey, That's Unbecoming

I love Jesus. I really do. But don't call me religious. It makes my blood boil.

Also, I watch *The Housewives,* and I'm not sorry.

I didn't grow up going to a Bible church. I didn't wear a purity ring. I didn't spend summers at Christian camp, and I didn't have a pastor in skinny jeans and cool sneakers. I was raised Catholic. Priests wore robes. There were no rock bands up front or fog machines. What's with the fog machines?

When I was young and learning about God, there was a thoughtfulness to it all, a studiousness. It often felt like an intellectual endeavor. I love this about Catholicism. All the history, the art, the contemplative traditions. To this day, my favorite writers are Catholic priests: Brennan Manning, Henri Nouwen, Richard Rohr, and Thomas Merton. I love to read anything spiritual. So, at this point, I've read hundreds of books about faith written by men and women, and I learn something new every time. But nothing grips my heart like the words of Brennan Manning in *The Ragamuffin Gospel.* I'll share one quote here, but for the love of God, if you haven't read it, order it today.

> "Define yourself radically as one beloved by God.
> This is the true self. Every other identity is an illusion."
> —Brennan Manning

Your identity is this: Beloved Child of God.

Don't complicate things.

This is our starting point. The very foundation that we build our lives upon.

The Catholic church wasn't talking about that. It was more about doing the right thing, don't mess up, prove you love God by behaving your way into His good graces.

My mom was raised Baptist so that created a unique spin on the whole religion thing for me personally. What this amounts to when we were much younger is that:

1. My mom is loving and kind, and *always* puts her lipstick on before leaving the house and certainly before church.

2. My mom said, "Honey, that's unbecoming" *a lot.* This is good and bad. (I feel like it could be a whole other book). But the truth is, lots of stuff *is* unbecoming. She's not wrong. I said it to my kids too because, frankly, that's such a good word, and now they say it which is odd because it's old-fashioned. It makes me laugh. But it makes me proud too because they always perfectly place it, *knowing* some things are just...well, unbecoming. I raised them well. And all the Baptist church ladies said, "A-MEN!"

3. My mom has a gorgeous voice and knows all the hymns. So we often got side-eye when the music would start at Mass, and she just couldn't get pumped up about the

organ and the songs that sound like a funeral dirge on a Sunday morning in spring. We also heard her opinion that the crucifix was "focusing on death," and we are "Easter people," full of hope and promise. Why can't we just have a cross up front?

4. Also, you don't need to go to confession with a priest to be forgiven by God. You can just ask for forgiveness. Straight line to JC. Priests as middlemen and saints as intercessors are not necessary. I never really prayed to saints. Except when I was older, I learned to pray to Tony (Saint Anthony). He helped us find stuff. "Tony, Tony, look around, something's lost and can't be found." Oh, and maybe there was a St. Joseph statue buried upside down in the yard when we were trying to sell the house, but I can't confirm.

So these are the things I think about.

Spiritual ideas and concepts like freedom and redemption and reconciliation and sanctification and grace and mercy, spin in my mind. I seek out these themes. I always have. I'm also interested in shame and guilt and behavior modification and fear and our thought life and the danger of believing lies and why we all feel like caged animals when Jesus came to set us free!

And why did He do that? And what does that mean for me? And why didn't I learn this in the pews as a kid, and what should I do with this *knowing* now that I know?

This is what lights a fire in me.

I love stories of the lost being found. The shackles coming off. The captive being set free. This is every Jesus story.

I used to think it was for people like the disciples or Joseph and his brothers or Noah. Or the characters etched in stained glass or painted on canvas in Italy somewhere. I used to see it all as a story to learn, facts to know, knowledge to tuck away so you had that whole redemption thing figured out but didn't talk about it at parties. Because, well...unbecoming.

But when I really got that it was for *me*, and for my husband, my kids, my friends—I didn't care about what was appropriate at the dinner table. I had to tell people! This was personal and life- changing and meant to be shared! It was such a relief. Such a glorious exhale! I wanted to share it with everyone. "Lay your burdens down!" I wanted to shout from the rooftops.

It has been a process. A pruning if you will. Which is why I'm certain God made me wait until now to write a book. I used to come in hot. Or should we say, when I was younger, I was feistier in my delivery. I had the mistaken idea that I needed to convince everyone around me that Jesus is the answer! I needed them to agree with me. I had to make a case for Jesus. I needed to save people. (Just typing that makes me cringe.)

One night I was sitting around a table with a few people, and I was presenting the case for Jesus, complete with arguments and counterarguments. Like a total jerk. Probably pushing people *away* from Jesus. A friend of mine said gently but firmly, "Sue, Jesus doesn't need an attorney."

Full stop.

Duh.

Of course, I know I can't save people; the Holy Spirit does that. I can share my story, but who the heck did I think I was *arguing* about grace and love?

My pastor says, "Nobody is argued into the kingdom. They are loved in."

I want to be a witness for the way grace is all around us. Whether we are drinking coffee in our kitchen, waiting in the carpool line at school, walking in a park, dancing on tables in a bar, anticipating an important call, dining at a restaurant, signing divorce papers, recovering in a hospital room, panicking at an interview, flying on an airplane, promising at the altar, recovering in rehab, crying in our car, sweating the gym...wherever we are, God is with us.

There is not a place you go that God is not there.

There is not a feeling you feel that He does not know.

It's less about religion and more about a personal relationship with Jesus. I know that really freaks some people out. They are fine talking about God but when you start talking about Jesus, they get squirrely.

But then there comes a time in your life when you feel alone, scared, hopeless, or at the end of your rope. Your coping mechanisms no longer work. You realize that doing it in your own strength has limits and you have reached them. Where do you go?

There is not one religion that has everything right. That's why I don't want to label myself anything but a Jesus follower. Keeping my eyes on Him helps me remember that I really don't know much.

Two quotes come to mind:

> **"If you understood him, it would not be God."**
> —St. Augustine of Hippo

> **"You can safely assume you've created God in your own image when it turns out that God hates all the same people you do."** —Anne Lamott

Let's not act like we have all the answers. It's annoying.

I go to a huge Bible church in Texas now. I'm still not a fan of the fog machines. And it seems just plain wrong to take communion from a plastic cup, peeling off the foil top to get to the grape juice. I mean shouldn't we be kneeling? Where's the reverence here? But then the pastor will focus on the message of grace and redemption and the Bible will be open in his hands while he speaks. I'll leave there feeling simultaneously hugged and slapped, grateful that God led me to this place at this time.

None of it is wasted. All of it matters.

Let God lead you through the hallowed halls of Catholic cathedrals and into the junior high gym where a new church is being planted. Let Him walk you through the stations of the cross etched in stained glass windows and to a blanket on the lawn at an outside church service. Follow Him to the foot of the cross with the generations that came before you, some holding rosaries and prayer books from their Italian mothers and Irish fathers, and then follow Him to the ocean where the next generation is being baptized.

Read what the monks wrote and meditate on the Word of God and then write your own prayers in your journal, trusting God's voice and the gift of the Holy Spirit within you. Etch the Beatitudes on the tablet of your heart, recite God's prayer, and when you are really desperate, ask St. Anthony to help you find your lost keys.

Kneel in front of the altar and beg for forgiveness or just meet with God in the privacy of your own home and tell Him you are sorry. Just show up. Pay attention. And raise your hands in joyful hymns of praise. With or without the fog machine.

* What is your faith background?
* Where has God led you to learn more about Him?
* What in your past has helped you trust God for your future?

I Go to Church
to Pray, Not to Play

My dad passed away when I was only twenty-eight years old. For my whole life, he was my hero. I had placed him way up on a pedestal. At his Catholic funeral, one moment stands out for me. There were several priests up on the altar, and they kept referring to him as, "Brother John."

At that moment, I immediately saw my dad differently. He was not a hero to be worshiped. He was an imperfect but exceptionally amazing man, a Christian brother, on this journey with me. He was not without flaws; he was in need of a Savior like the rest of us.

He was my dad, yes, but in a larger sense, he is *my brother in Christ.* This was a fundamental shift for me that helped me see everyone, regardless of age or rank or status, as a brother or sister who is on this same journey with me, broken, in need of a Savior, and doing the best they can.

Gosh, sometimes I miss the formality of the Catholic church. The formal language and the rituals and the reverence of it all. It sticks with you.

But it's not all so serious.

I mean, there's nothing like St. Paddy's Day in Chicago. Green river, big parade, day drinking. And also in Chicago, in my twenties when

I lived in Lincoln Park, there was nothing like an Old St. Pat's block party in the summer. We had so much fun!

I have lots of stories of CCD on Wednesday nights, and church lady casseroles in the basement of the church. I went to CCD for the express purpose of looking at boys. One in particular. I couldn't wait to go! I would curl my bangs in one big curl with my curling iron and tease the rest of it with Aqua Net.

Before I left, my dad would quiz me, "Who made the world?"

I would have to say, "God made the world," in a full sentence. I couldn't say, "God" because that would be lazy. My dad was an educated, well-spoken man. He didn't approve of "Yeah." It had to be "Yes." Because "Yeah" is lazy, and, frankly, it's unbecoming.

When it came to mass, there was no joking around. One time my brothers were horsing around in church, and my dad made them write one-hundred times, "I go to church to pray, not to play." My oldest brother, being the salesman he was born to be, talked the neighbor into writing this for him. He sold him on how "fun it would be."

When I think of our childhood shenanigans, I can see so clearly all our original designs shining through. We are who God made us to be. And rightly so. I can hear God saying, "Shine, child! Shine your light!" Some of us shine through humor, some negotiate, some stay in the background, some are good listeners, some are intelligent, some are creative.

A lot of our lives are spent trying to be something we are not. And unfortunately, for a lot of us, church can be one of the big reasons we pretend. We try to fit a certain mold we think is proper and "right" for a Christian, instead of just coming before Jesus and being real. We have to allow Him to love us as we are and not hide until we feel presentable. We are all works in progress. But He wants to love us now. He is not waiting for some future version of us to be "good enough."

> "'Are you tired? Worn out? Burned out on religion? Come to me. Get away with me and you'll recover your life. I'll show you how to take a real rest. Walk with me and work with me—watch how I do it. Learn the unforced rhythms of grace. I won't lay anything heavy or ill-fitting on you. Keep company with me and you'll learn to live freely and lightly.'" (Matthew 11:28-30 MSG)

"Unforced rhythms of grace." Isn't that magnificent?

That's what we are getting at when we tell our true, beautiful, unique stories. We don't have to perform, pretend, and manufacture.

We can breathe. He is here, every day of our lives. At funerals and parades and block parties and regular Sunday mornings. He is with us when we pray, and He is with us when we play.

* Who do you need to take off a pedestal and recognize as a brother or sister in Christ?
* What memories of church do you have from your childhood?
* In what ways do you pretend before the Lord?

It's Okay

When I was in grade school, something happened that I don't remember but my mom told me about it, and it has always stuck with me. I grew up in the Midwest, so we had cold winters. This means when you are at school and heading out for recess, it's a whole process to put on coats, gloves, hats, and boots. One time in third grade, my teacher was helping me zip up my coat and the zipper broke. He felt terrible and kept apologizing. I said, "It's okay. My mom won't be mad."

He relayed this story to my mom, but she didn't tell me about it until I was older. It's interesting that my mom thought it was an important story. I think it is too. It shows a couple of things. One, I was raised by a great mom. She didn't sweat the small stuff. She didn't get angry and fly off the handle. She was kind (still is!) and generous of spirit. She would never want to make anyone feel bad. She was proud of me at this moment because I offered my teacher grace. I let him off the hook.

I couldn't have explained grace or kindness at that young age, but I knew it because my mom taught me, just by the way she lived.

I want to be that kind of mom.

When we moved to Texas after a lifetime of living in Illinois, with a 6th, 9th, and 11th grader, I tried to just roll with whatever was going on. It was tough. I said, "It's okay" to the kids a lot. I showed up, met people, asked questions, laughed, stayed open, and tried to manage my expectations. All along, saying to my kids, "It's okay" and trying not to fly off the handle at the little things. I tried not to worry or project into the future or wonder if this was all a big mistake.

One day, during our first months in Texas, I went grocery shopping at HEB. (For all y'all not from here, you need to know, shopping at HEB is an experience.) The refrigerator was loaded to the max. I opened the door to get something out and strawberries and blueberries flew everywhere! I was not calm. I yelled, "OH NO-NO-NO!"

You know what happened?

All three of my kids came running. They saw me on the floor, and they got down with me to pick up the fruit. They said, "It's okay, Mom," "It's no big deal, Mom," "Don't worry. We can wash the fruit, Mom." I couldn't have been prouder at that moment. Or more grateful.

I will remind them of that story one day.

The way they offered me kindness and grace and understanding.

It was just a tiny moment, but to me, it was huge.

It's no small thing to tell your kids, "It's okay." One day they will say it back to you, just when you need to hear it most.

* What did your parents teach you by their example?
* How has your relationship with God helped you relate to people?
* In what ways are you good at offering grace?

Brave Conversations

"Do you think you'll go to heaven?"

When I was a teenager, my friend asked me this. His dad was a Baptist preacher. Since I was raised Catholic, I had never been asked this before.

I said, "Sure!"

He asked why.

I confidently answered, "Because I'm a good person."

I'll never forget it. I can still see what he was wearing and where we were standing.

When people tell you the Truth, you remember.

He boldly and kindly said, "You don't get into heaven by being a good person. You have to ask Jesus into your heart."

Although I'd never heard this before, it rang true. His words immediately seized my heart.

I began seeking. Asking questions. I wish I could say I was pursuing Jesus, but I recognize now that I was pursuing knowledge.

Who is right?

Why didn't my church tell me this?

What does this mean for me?

How do I go about "asking Jesus into my heart"?

I've never stopped asking and seeking. It's a lifelong journey. As I've gotten older, my search for knowledge has turned into a search for peace. I long for freedom from anxiety, fear, and the need to control. And as God would have it, each step, each question, all my time seeking has led me directly into the arms of Jesus.

I remember once talking to someone about being "born again." I was in my thirties, and she was probably in her sixties. She was Catholic and I was sharing this experience with her, getting her take on the whole situation. I asked her if she thought we needed to be "born again." She said, "Oh, honey, if you could only know how many times I've been 'born again'..."

That stuck with me.

The more I live, the more I realize that asking Him into my heart is a daily thing. Asking Him into my life, kitchen, work, bedroom, car, marriage, writing, family, scrolling, watching, listening, thinking, breathing. It's a conscious choice every day to walk with Him, the Prince of Peace.

I think back to that specific moment on my basement stairs in the 1980s, pool table below us, shag rug underneath. My friend was wearing a flannel shirt, standing confidently in his belief, willing to have a brave conversation, and he planted a seed that changed my life. I'm forever grateful.

* Do you think you are going to heaven?
* Who first shared Jesus with you?
* When has a conversation changed your path?

Rules vs. Relationship

So much of our life is about learning to follow the rules. School, church, family, and society all have a particular set of rules we learn to follow. This reminds me of something I heard once. We were in an assembly at the high school for teens and parents, learning the do's and don'ts of internet etiquette. The speaker suggested a good rule of thumb. Before you post anything, ask yourself, *Would I say this or show this to my parents, my pastor, the principal, and the police?* If not, don't post it. This is good advice.

But when we decide that the rules are a prerequisite for love, then we are all mixed up.

Your parents don't love you because you follow a strict set of rules. I can honestly say as a mom, my greatest joy and sense of a job well done as a parent, doesn't come when my kids act like they are perfect or when they appear perfect to the outside world. I feel the proudest of my parenting when they come to me honestly and they trust me with the truth, when they share their heart with me unfiltered, trusting me to love them in the messiness.

This is God with us. It's about relationships. Sure, there are rules, but we will break them. It's a fact. Good thing our salvation doesn't depend on us being perfect. We are saved by God's grace.

So when the church says you have to do this or that for God to love you, that's not true.

> "For it is by grace you have been saved, through faith—
> and this is not from yourselves, it is the gift of God—
> not by works, so that no one can boast."
>
> (Ephesians 2:8-9 NIV)

Grace is "unmerited favor." So, there is no way you can earn it. This is good news. In fact, it's THE GOOD NEWS. Receiving the saving grace you seek, the grace that leads to eternal life and the grace that surrounds you here on earth, the grace that allows you to live freely and lightly, has nothing to do with your good works. It's not about following rules or jumping through hoops to complete paperwork and attend ceremonies and check boxes.

My pastor puts it this way: It's "Jesus plus nothing." It's not Jesus plus confirmation or Jesus plus the rosary or Jesus plus five Hail Marys and two Our Fathers. If it was dependent on your good works, then what about the thief on the cross next to Jesus?

> "One of the criminals who hung there hurled insults at him: 'Aren't you the Messiah? Save yourself and us!' But the other criminal rebuked him. 'Don't you fear God,' he said, 'since you are under the same sentence? We are punished justly, for we are getting what our deeds deserve. But this man has done nothing wrong.' Then he said, 'Jesus, remember me when you come into your kingdom.' Jesus answered him, 'Truly I tell you, today you will be with me in paradise.'" (Luke 23:39-43 NIV)

Jesus didn't say, "Well, if only you had time to go through baptism classes" or "Are you confirmed?" or "Have you taken communion?" or "When was your last confession?"

He just said *yes*. He said *today*.

No waiting period. No trial run. No consulting with your neighbors. No checking your status in the church. No, "Well, you blew it because you didn't go to Mass that Sunday you were on vacation in 1992."

He will not reject you. But it's not because you are so good. It's because He is.

* What do you need to confess to God?

* What are you trying to control with regard to your own salvation?

* In what ways do you need to forgive yourself?

Fight or Flight or Faith

In November of 1994, I was held up at gunpoint.

I lived in Chicago. I was walking alone at night. A man with a gun came up, pointed the gun at me, and said, "Give me your bag." I gave him my bag, and then I ran as fast as I could.

It changed everything.

For months after that, I went through a transformative experience. At the time, I didn't know what was happening to me. I couldn't get on the "El" or a city bus without being completely out of breath and shaking. Several times, I thought I was having a heart attack, and I literally couldn't breathe. There were times when my chin or my arm would go numb. Certain I was dying, I made several trips to the ER to have CAT scans and EEGs and EKGs.

Two really important things happened at this time. I was talking to my mom about it, and I was really freaked out. I was not sure what was happening to me, but I knew that I was not okay. She said to me, "Have you prayed about it?"

No, I had not prayed about it. I had talked about it with everyone, I had seen many doctors, and I had tried to fix it myself, but I had not prayed about it. I read books and sought advice from friends. (This was 1994 so there were no podcasts, but I'm certain I would have been consulting those as well.) I went to everyone who I thought could fix it, and I didn't go to the One who actually could. It was an *"aha* moment," My mom, again, was wise and faithful.

That moment stands as a turning point in my life and in my walk of faith.

The other really important thing that happened was that I went to a doctor many times hoping for answers, getting tests, often just hoping she would give me "something" to take away the symptoms. I wanted a magic pill to make it all go away. So much has changed for me since 1994. While now I would not seek a pill to save me, this happened when I knew nothing about mental health or holistic healing. At the time, I was desperate. I most certainly would have welcomed a prescription.

However, God had other plans. This was a divine fork in the road of my life. It didn't feel divine; it felt like hell. It was confusing and scary and isolating, and I was filled with fear. But God.

"But God" is always a miraculous phrase in the Bible. When we read that, we should sit up and take note. Anything is possible with God. We have plans, "but God." We have fear, "but God." We don't see a way out, "but God."

God led me to a doctor who was enlightened. She took the time to ask me what had been going on in my life. I started rambling off a list of things. I told her I just got married, I just got mugged... she stopped me there.

She asked for details, and we talked about what happened. Then she pulled her chair closer and said, "You have PTSD. You are having panic attacks. Your body senses that it is in danger because your mind is telling it so. Your body is reacting with a fight-or-flight response. Your mind is tricking your body into this reaction.

Your mind and body are intricately linked. We need to address the mind and the fear in order to stop the panic attacks."

Then she taught me how to breathe. She essentially taught me yoga breath. She told me I should practice this breath to calm my central nervous system. I practiced this breath as I was facing my fears on public transportation and while walking alone. It helped me so much that my panic attacks were mostly gone. When they would return, I would "check-in" with my mind and then begin my breath. I would tell myself, "At this moment, I am not in danger." This was the beginning of my walk with mindfulness.

Now that I have been in ministry for a while, I know that the word mindfulness can make some Christians nervous. Here is the definition of mindfulness that I am thinking of here: *a mental state achieved by focusing one's awareness on the present moment, while calmly acknowledging and accepting one's feelings, thoughts, and bodily sensations, used as a therapeutic technique.*

For example, you notice that your heart is racing. You feel panicky and you can't get a deep enough breath. By focusing on being present in the moment, you can say, *Wow, I am having a reaction here. I must be afraid. But right now, at the moment, I am okay. I am safe. I am going to take a deep, deliberate breath. I don't have to rush. I am okay. Lord, be with me and help me in this moment. Bring me peace.* This conscious focus on the present moment, while accepting and noticing what's happening in your body, helps stop the cycle. The breath work literally calms the central nervous system. God created us with a body, mind, and soul and they are all intricately linked.

At that time, this became my life verse.

"Do not be anxious about anything, but in every situation, by prayer and petition, with thanksgiving, present your requests to God. And the peace of God, which transcends all understanding, will guard your hearts and your minds in Christ Jesus."

(Philippians 4:6-7 NIV)

God and my breath saved me from my panic attacks.

Let's talk about breath for a minute and how overlooked it is as a healing tool. God breathed life into us. I can't separate myself from my breath. Therefore, I know God is always with me. His breath is my breath. If I feel anxious, I can just return to my breath. If I don't know what to pray, I just breathe, intentionally and slowly, and I listen. Breathing is connecting to God, our source of power and peace.

How ironic that in the middle of what could be the worst thing that has happened to me, I learned two things that now define me.

1. **Rely on God.** What matters to me matters to Him. Talk to Him. Pray. He is capable and can do anything. He is the Healer I need with the answers I seek.

2. **Be mindful.** The mind and body are intricately linked. Take care of both. Be present and in the moment. Do not fear. Breathe.

In 2012 I became a certified yoga instructor. I taught from a Christian perspective, so I had the opportunity to offer the life-giving breath work, meditation, and movement of yoga with the saving grace of Jesus. I was able to teach others about the things that gave me my life back.

Eventually, I was trained to teach "Trauma Sensitive Yoga." I remember learning about what trauma does to the body, and although it was twenty-five years after my attack, I could feel it. I understood what I was learning because I had lived it. I found myself teaching Trauma Sensitive Yoga to young women under the age of nineteen who had been victims of sex trafficking. This is a "But God" story. He took one of the most horrific, terrifying things that happened to me and used it for good. Twenty-five years later, I sat weeping in a class about trauma and yoga and Jesus, realizing that He orchestrated that very moment, that full circle moment, *for me.*

> "And we know that for those who love God all things work together for good, for those who are called according to his purpose." (Romans 8:28 ESV)

If you are going through something really hard, if you are challenged and dismayed and discouraged and scared, ask Jesus for help. He will comfort you. It may be a word He gives you; it may be through the transforming of your mind; it may be a reminder to return to your breath. He will lead you to people who will help you on your healing path. He comforts us individually and uniquely. And one day, He may invite you to comfort and encourage others. You will be ready.

> "He comforts us in all our troubles so that we can comfort others. When they are troubled, we will be able to give them the same comfort God has given us."
> (2 Corinthians 1:4 NLT)

* How has God comforted you? How has He asked you to comfort others?

* What are some tools for healing that you have learned in your life?

* Looking back, what was a "fork in the road" of your life?

Joy Stories

stars light up the night. big Texas sky covers us graciously. tucking us in for a story. campfire burns. we stare. mesmerized by light and warmth. notes play as voices sing. sharing loss and desire. we understand each other. universal stories. contentment. joyful noise.

he reaches out for my hand as we walk. stomach flutters. unsure of what's next. heart beating in my throat. hoping he'll tell me who he is. what he loves. where he hurts. eager to be let in. listening intently. story unfolding. joy coming.

bright lights. lots of people. noise. doctors racing. nurses talking. my feet are cold. searing pain. fear. hurry. worry. wait. wonder. why. there will be no cry they say. do not be afraid. clean out mouth and take away...trusting. listening. it's okay they say. scared. mom? who is here? what time is it? so much pain. hear a cry. relief. tears. laughter. joy delivered.

big tree with tire swing. golf carts and trampoline. bikes against the fence. hoop too high for me. brother lifts me. leaves crunch. hide and seek. running. pool. stories. who said what. who did what. who do you like. where are you going. friends. laughter. long lazy days of summer. joy remembered.

entering in. unrolling my mat. movement. deep cleansing breaths. stillness. meditation. inner journey. awakening. light. calm. peace. community. safety. wellness. health. grace. prayer. new life. joyful freedom.

These are just some of my Joy Stories. I have asked God to give me more joy in my original design...more joy in who He has made me to be...more joy in my unique story.

Joy is our birthright and our destiny. We must claim it. Own it.

It is trendy now to talk about what's "wrong," and the ways you are struggling. On social media, there is a lot of whining and complaining and acting the victim. Without question, there is a time and a place for a sincere discussion about the challenges we face personally and collectively. However, this culture of victimhood is not our inheritance. God has more for us. We have to decide to believe it and then live like we believe it! I don't mean we should be fake, and I don't believe in the toxic positivity of "good vibes only." However, I do believe our thoughts have a big impact on our lives. We hear about this from life coaches, therapists, philosophers, new-age gurus, Instagram influencers, and great writers.

"The mind is its own place and, in itself, can make a heaven of hell or a hell of heaven." —John Milton

We also hear about it in God's Word.

> "For though we live in the world, we do not wage war as the world does. The weapons we fight with are not the weapons of the world. On the contrary, they have divine power to demolish strongholds. We demolish arguments and every pretension that sets itself up against the knowledge of God, and we take captive every thought to make it obedient to Christ."
>
> (2 Corinthians 10:3-5 NIV)

If we know God's character, if we spend time with Him in prayer and in His Word, if we have a relationship with Him, then we can tell what "sets itself up against the knowledge of God." So when we think, "I'm not smart enough, I'm not fit enough, I can't do it, I have no future, no one likes me, I have no gifts, I can't trust God," and any other myriad of lies we may tell ourselves, we have to be able to stop, take that thought captive and ask, "Is this true?" "Would God say this?" When we practice this, we can weed out the lies of the world that kill and destroy and rely on the promises of God who gives life to the full.

> "'The thief comes only to steal and kill and destroy; I have come that they may have life, and have it to the full.'"
> (John 10:10 NIV)

We can also see the lies in the arguments of other people. If the world comes at us and attacks our beliefs or confuses us or causes chaos in our minds, we can consult God and call out the lies. This takes practice and knowledge of who God is and what He says. Throughout our lives, we will have to fight voices and influences, within and without, that may tell us we are not worthy, but God equips us to stand secure in His love.

Joy is a fruit of the Spirit. It's a deeper fullness that can only come from God. It's not circumstantial. You can still be a joyful person when you are in the midst of a tough season in life. I think of the words, "It is well with my soul." There is an assurance that all will be well because there is a sovereign God who loves us and calls us by name. The world does not give joy. It may give temporary happiness, but it will also take it away. Joy is always in you, a gift from God. However, there are moments when you will feel it more acutely.

When have you experienced joy?

Let's tell that story.

 * Try writing your own poem of joy, modeled after mine.
 * When have you experienced joy?
 * Who do you know that is a joyful person?

Uncool

One time I was sitting around with a group of people, and we were sharing our most embarrassing stories. I was telling them about the time an old boyfriend was leaving me. Literally. We were at the airport, and he broke up with me right before getting on a plane to actually leave. I was begging him not to go. I was crying and at one point resorted to hanging on his leg. He was mortified and was trying to get me off him.

The whole thing was so uncool. Living it and telling it. Doubly uncool.

He didn't change his mind. He left. I was devastated. I mean, it's okay; it all worked out. Of course, I know now that he wasn't supposed to stay.

My favorite line from Lester Banks in the movie *Almost Famous* is, "The only true currency in this bankrupt world is what we share with someone else when we're uncool."

Amen.

Who have you ever been "uncool" with? Are you always "uncool"? And I mean this in the best sense of the word, meaning, not self-conscious, not pretending.

Or the opposite? Do you walk into a room and chameleon yourself into whatever you need to be to be cool in that space?

I've done both.

Have you ever met someone who is so completely themselves, so utterly free, that you just can't be anything other than real? I love those people. They are few and far between. When you find them, you've got to hang on.

It's fun to be uncool. But it can be scary too.

At least we grew up without social media. I'm worried about this younger generation because they never see anyone being uncool. It's all photoshopped and filtered. Anything that's not flattering or "on brand" gets deleted. And along with it, goes the possibility for real connection.

Real connection is what we all want, right?

As I was sharing that embarrassing story with the group, people were chuckling, and I could tell they might have even had second-hand embarrassment. But one guy spoke up. I remember it to this day. He said, "I don't think that's embarrassing; I think it's real. It shows that you know how to love another person fully and completely. That's actually amazing."

And there you have it. The power of being uncool.

- ✳ When have you been uncool?
- ✳ When have you hidden in shame because of being uncool?
- ✳ When have you connected with someone because of your awkwardness or vulnerability?

Come as You Are

This is the invitation.

Come as you are.

Don't hesitate. Bring all your messy, confused, imperfect, joyful, doubtful, seeking, loving, authentic self. Bring the part of you that is scared. Bring your heart that is broken. Bring your worries and bring your joys. Bring you. Bring your laughter and your quirky sense of humor. Bring your relationships and your habits and your personality and all the things that make you who you are.

There is nothing you can say or do or show Jesus that will scare Him off. He wants you.

He doesn't want a performance or a perfect answer. He doesn't demand that you jump through forty hoops to get to Him. There is no secret passcode or VIP list you have to get your name on. You don't need the approval of others.

This is the difference between religion and relationship. The point isn't to know *about* Jesus—the point is to actually *know* Jesus. He invites us into the deep work of a trusting, committed relationship that is constantly being renewed. He invites us into friendship and intimacy and that is sacred, holy ground.

What will happen if you show up as you are? He will open your eyes and your heart. If need be, He will break down walls of pride and fear and years of clinging to how right you think you are. He will make you vulnerable. And once you are standing there naked, stripped of all you think you know, He will love you. He will set a path before you that you could never imagine on your own.

You will be free.

One of my favorite things written by Brennan Manning is this. It takes my breath away every time.

> *"Because salvation is by grace through faith, I believe that among the countless number of people standing in front of the throne and in front of the Lamb, dressed in white robes and holding palms in their hands (see Revelation 7:9), I shall see the prostitute from the Kit-Kat Ranch in Carson City, Nevada, who tearfully told me that she could find no other employment to support her two-year-old son. I shall see the woman who had an abortion and is haunted by guilt and remorse but did the best she could faced with grueling alternatives; the businessman besieged with debt who sold his integrity in a series of desperate transactions; the insecure clergyman addicted to being liked, who never challenged his people from the pulpit and longed for unconditional love; the sexually abused teen molested by his father and now selling his body on the street, who, as he falls asleep each night after his last 'trick', whispers the name of the unknown God he learned about in Sunday school.*
>
> *"'But how?' we ask.*

"Then the voice says, 'They have washed their robes and have made them white in the blood of the Lamb.'

"There they are. There we are—the multitude who so wanted to be faithful, who at times got defeated, soiled by life, and bested by trials, wearing the bloodied garments of life's tribulations, but through it all clung to faith.

"My friends, if this is not good news to you, you have never understood the gospel of grace."

That is the invitation. Come as you are...and leave transformed.

✳ Have you experienced freedom in Christ? What does that mean to you?

✳ Do you hesitate to go to God with your full self?

✳ What parts of you do you think you need to clean up before God will love you?

Big Red F

"All serious daring starts from within." —Eudora Welty

Many kids attend some type of leadership training when they are in junior high or high school or college. I always loved those retreats. The dictionary says *to lead* is to be "in command" or "to guide someone or take someone somewhere."

Does the "where" have to be physical?

Does the leading have to be linked to accomplishment and success?

Think of Jesus. He was a leader. He led us to the cross. Hmmm... success? Now we know the rest of the story, but if we didn't know about Easter, was He a failure or a success in life? What about Martin Luther King? He led us to turmoil and conflict, and He was murdered. Success? Of course, now we know his legacy, but do you think he was familiar with failure?

The dictionary doesn't say where you are leading someone. It doesn't say you are leading them to climb the mountain or win the race or be loved by everyone. It says you are leading them somewhere. Can that somewhere be intellectual or emotional or spiritual?

When I think of great leaders in my life, I don't immediately go to football or basketball coaches. Our society tends to focus on sports and many leaders are born on the field or in the gym, no doubt. Politics comes up when we think of leadership too and the military and business. But I want to talk about a different kind of leader.

I want to talk about teachers. Particularly the ones in classrooms.

I remember hearing a quote once that a doctor has the ability to save a life one person at a time, but a teacher has the chance to save thirty lives at a time. If they have the power to save lives, what else do they have the power to do? Really. It's that serious.

I had an amazing teacher in 4th grade. He was demanding and funny and creative and kind. He taught 3rd, 4th, and 5th grades together, and he pushed all sorts of limits. It was the 70s so you can imagine. We were trying all kinds of experimental things including school meetings in the new "pod" which was groovy. It was a huge open room with no walls that hosted several classes of mixed grades. Only partitions divided the spaces. Did you have those? It's funny how education goes through these phases. New math, whole language, open classrooms. God be with those of us who were part of these experiments! I can't imagine how difficult it would be if you had ADHD to concentrate in a huge open space like that. I'm sure that was not education's best moment. But it was the 70s, so...

This teacher was especially cool to the kids. He was hilarious. He made a little clay figure like "Mr. Bill" on *Saturday Night Live* and "Mr. Bill" would have all sorts of classroom adventures.

He loved to read to us out loud even though we could read ourselves. One time, he read *The Amityville Horror* to us (so scary!). He was always cutting-edge and unique and out of the box. I'm sure he was pushing the administrator's buttons constantly. He sang, he danced, and he laughed a lot. I can imagine him laughing now. He was engaged. He loved learning, and he loved teaching. He made school come alive for me and many other kids.

On my first test in his class, I got an F, a 32%. I was devastated. I had never gotten anything other than an A. I was crying. I will never forget what he said to me. He got on his knees in front of my little chair, and he looked right into my eyes. He said, "I would rather have you get all Fs and be challenged than have you get As for the rest of your life and never be challenged."

He was a leader. And he developed his students into leaders.

Because of his words, I am not afraid of an F. I am not afraid of something not working out. I'm not afraid to try. I'm not saying I still don't cry sometimes when I fail; I just know it will be okay. I'm not saying I don't hesitate sometimes or second guess myself, but I don't let fear get the best of me.

He led me to acceptance and courage and confidence. I'm not afraid to ask questions or be embarrassed when I don't know because I realize that's how I learn. I think this came from my experience with him. With each failing try in my life, I have learned something.

I recently heard a graduation speaker tell the graduates that in life, it's not about *not failing*. It's about failing better next time.

"Success consists of going from failure to failure without loss of enthusiasm." —Winston Churchill

Are we concerned more with the A than with the challenge? Are we trying to be so perfect, we aren't growing or learning? Are we demanding perfection of others?

We can give our kids all kinds of experiences on the outside. They can climb and run and jump and win, but can they fail? And when they do, do they have a leader near them, a parent, friend, teacher, or relative (you!) telling them they are great and brilliant and wonderful and important even when they don't succeed?

You can take all the young people (and you) all over the world, spend lots of money, hire many trainers, and still not have a leader on your hands. Because leadership does, in fact, start within. Turns out what's best for your kids has nothing to do with money or external experiences. It is about internal strength. How ironic. Winning is about failing...early and often.

Maybe we should ask teachers before we hire them, "How many times have you failed?" Then we may be able to tell if we are dealing with a leader.

What about you? Fail much?

* Who has been a good leader in your life?
* When have you failed?
* What have you learned from your failures?

GRACE AS
MY GUIDE

*Lord, thank you for our kids. Thanks for the hard
and holy gift of parenting. It brings us closer to
You because, oh boy, do we need You as we are
raising our kids. Lord, they teach us so much about
ourselves. As we look at the years of building
a family, raising children, and setting the tone
in our home, help us have grace for ourselves. I
pray that if we see things we wish we'd handled
differently, we keep the lessons learned but leave
the guilt and shame behind. Help us see the joy
and remember the laughter.*

It's a high honor to be called to be a parent. All kids are your kids. We are blessed to have the chance to steward them for a while.

There are so many big things like holidays and vacations and accomplishments, but it's the little stuff I'm thinking of now. Movie nights and catching fireflies. Bath time and books before bed. Clifford. Goodnight Moon. Arthur. Thomas the Tank Engine.

I'm remembering those days. The kids were little, and it was summer. It was happy hour, and we were barefoot on the driveway drinking wine. We just got back from the pool, still in swimsuits and cover-ups. The kids were running from the trampoline to the sandbox, to the swings, begging for money for the ice cream truck. Neighbors gathered with us, walking over with their kids. We would order pizza and stay there until the fireflies came out. Dirty feet, laughter, people in and out through the open back door. There was a glow. Or maybe that's just how I see it now. Golden hour. Golden season. A golden life.

Thank you, Lord. Amen.

The Cadillac Birth

Birthing my oldest child was hell. Honestly, it was over twenty-four hours of labor, and I had every intervention. They broke my water and gave me Pitocin. I had an epidural, and they had to perform a vacuum extraction. My doctor called it a "Cadillac Birth." This child was two weeks late so I had to be induced, and they told me she wouldn't cry right away because they had to take her away to wipe the poop out of her mouth before she could cry. So that's fun.

I was in the middle of it all when I heard this voice, "Susan?" It was my mom. She had waited long enough, and no one told her what was going on, so she came to find me.

This was a teaching hospital in Chicago so picture lots of people in the room. At one point, my husband joked, "I'm going to go grab some people from the hallway and see if they want to come in here and examine my wife giving birth."

It was a full room, the doctor, a couple of nurses, a few students, my husband, and now my mom. Actually, she never came in. I yelled, "Mom, get out of here!" And I assume she just turned around and left.

Birthing my second child was easy. Four hours start to finish. The doctor strolled in off the golf course just in time to catch her after the nurse had done all the hard work.

When I had my third child, my mom was babysitting my girls and getting nervous that she hadn't heard anything. She consulted with my best friend, and they decided my mom should come to the hospital. I was in the suburbs in a room that was peaceful and quiet. One nurse, one doctor, and my husband, reading a book. Literally, he read a book while I gave birth.

At a moment of pause when the doctor wasn't in the room, I heard my mom's voice in the hallway. She was chatting with someone like she was at a cocktail party. Then she came into the room, sat down by the bed, and whispered excitedly, "Oh my gosh, your doctor looks like Paul Newman," all giddy and blushing. I'm like, don't mind me. Just trying to give birth here.

Now when my kids get snippy with me, I want to say, "Do you know what I went through to give birth to you?" and "Do you know what Grandma went through when I gave birth to you?"

My husband did not want to cut the umbilical cord. He was grossed out by all of it honestly. He would have been great back in the day when the dad just smoked cigars out in the hallway and waited to see the cleaned-up baby through the window in the nursery. I remember friends saying their husbands would never miss a doctor's appointment and would do things like rub their feet and belly with oil. This was not happening at my house. He's not that guy, and he doesn't like hospitals and blood. By the third child, the doctor (the one who looks like Paul Newman) forced him to cut the cord. He handed him the scissors and said, "You are doing this." So he did.

When the babies were born and actually at home with us, my husband was a rock star. He was so comfortable with the babies. He didn't get up in the night to feed them because he had to "go to work" and he "doesn't have boobs." I was fine with that. Makes perfect sense to me.

I had one friend who was incensed about it. She couldn't believe the audacity. "How dare he!" she exclaimed, incredulous. Honestly, it didn't bother me. We had to figure out what worked for us. So, I was up at night rocking the baby, and he made dinner every night. I did a midnight feeding, and he did the grocery shopping. He took the baby for walks in the stroller so I could nap. He put her in the Baby Bjorn and walked with her out in the Chicago fall wind because it's the only thing that would stop her from crying. We figured out our own rhythm.

My favorite book when I was pregnant was *The Girlfriend's Guide to Pregnancy*. It was hilarious and real and nonjudgmental. I felt seen. Her husband worked too! He couldn't be at every doctor's appointment either! There are lots of ways to be pregnant, have a baby, and raise a baby. The doctor who delivered my first child said, "The goal is a healthy child" and encouraged me to not be too attached to my expectations of how everything should go. This was good advice.

And Paul Newman, as he will be referred to from now on, told me just what I needed to hear when I went to see him postpartum. I was weeping and carrying on about how difficult breastfeeding was. He looked right in my eyes (his eyes were so blue!), and said, "You don't have to breastfeed. You can stop now if you want." Full stop. I was stunned. Is that allowed? He was so kind, so relaxed, so confident. He assured me, "Do what works for you."

* If you have a birthing story, write about it.

* What details stand out to you as you remember giving birth to or adopting your kids?

* Who are the people that played an important role in this part of your life?

I Hope You Fail

Many people say they want their kids to just be happy. I think that is setting the bar too low. I want so much more than that for my kids. Right now, I'm thinking about how I want them to be capable and strong and adaptable and resilient. So I wrote another list of things I want to tell my kids.

Some of this might surprise you. These aren't the words we often use when talking to other moms.

See, I want my kids to fail this year.

I want them to succeed as well, but I really want them to fail while they are still at home with me. I don't want them to fail school, but I want them to be challenged in life this year.

I believe the only way they can learn is through falling and getting back up. I won't be there to rescue them in college or their first job or their marriage, so I don't plan on rescuing them this year either. It's gonna hurt. Mostly me.

Kids are resilient and strong and creative and resourceful. But we won't ever know this (and neither will they!) if we don't let them struggle.

Oh, I've felt the temptation more than once to rescue my child, do their homework, call that teacher, call that other mom, or fight their battles. I've gotten involved. I've stuck my nose in. Sometimes it helps and sometimes it hurts. But mostly, it's a band-aid until the next problem comes up, and then I have to go in and rescue again because they didn't learn how to be self-sufficient the first time. Is this my children's fault? No, it's mine. I mistakenly thought that I was helping them, but I was unintentionally stunting their growth. I was limiting them. I was *hovering*.

I wrote some things I hope for my kids this year that I want to share with you.

I hope you get a teacher you don't like. Seriously, I hope you really don't like him in the beginning, but you end up respecting him in the end.

I hope you are afraid in speech class. And then I want you to show yourself how brave you are by getting up and speaking with a shaky voice. It might be terrible. And I want you to be okay with that because of the relief you feel that it's over. Then I want you to have that satisfied feeling that comes from doing something scary. I want you to know you *can* because you *did*.

I hope you have some unsure moments in the lunchroom. I hope you go up to the girl who is alone at lunch, and you smile, and you sit down, and you begin. Even when your heart is beating fast, and your head is doubting strong. I want you to be brave enough to begin.

I hope you are lonely sometimes, so you know how it feels and then I hope you make your mind up to invite others, so they don't have to feel that way. I want you to notice if they feel alone. I want you to *see* people. I want your eyes to be kind and your heart to be willing.

I hope you don't get what you want so you can realize that you may want some things you don't need.

I hope you feel that pit of nervousness in your stomach and you walk in anyway.

I hope you don't laugh when they are making fun of her. And I hope when they notice you not laughing, you tell them you're not laughing because it's not funny.

Then I hope you stand strong when they start making fun of you.

I hope you say no when you know it's not right, even when it means you will miss out.

I hope you miss out. And then I hope you realize you are glad you weren't there.

I hope you are betrayed by a friend. You will endure the pain and isolation and deep hurt that comes from this. Then you will know that true friendship is built on loyalty and trust. And knowing this, you will become that friend to people. You will be loyal and trustworthy.

I hope you are required to read a book you don't want to read, but then I hope you are moved, and you can relate and you feel your heart opening.

I hope you are forced outside of your comfort zone to meet someone new, someone different, someone you never noticed before, and then I hope you realize how much you enjoy being around him or her.

I hope you go through something emotionally challenging. I hope you are brave enough to be vulnerable and share your struggles with a friend. Then I hope you are rewarded with trust and understanding. I hope you experience some "You too? I thought it was just me!" moments.

I hope you realize you don't know everything.

I hope you get embarrassed and instead of putting up a wall of "acting cool," I hope you choose to just accept it and laugh instead.

I hope you don't know all the answers, and you ask the teacher for what you need even when you feel stupid and awkward and afraid.

I hope you try again.

I really do hope for these things. Because these are the things that help us grow. These are the things that make us realize we can do it. No matter what "it" is, we will be prepared because we have failed, and we have *survived*.

So, this year, you will see me *not hovering*. In fact, you may not see me. But I'll be here. I'll be watching and praying. I'll be listening, and I will be hugging and supporting and probably shedding more than one or two tears. We will be our flawed, not perfect, messy, struggling human selves over here at our house. We will be working hard, but you may not see it because this is internal work. We may not see the results for years.

Some people may think I'm not paying attention. That's okay. It's not about what other people think. It's about my kids. I want them to grow into the beautiful, mature, intelligent, and wise people God intends them to be. And that doesn't just happen. Sometimes you gotta let it hurt a little.

It hurts to grow up. And it especially hurts to do it a second time. But I'm getting there.

* How have you failed lately?
* What has failure taught you?
* What kind of a person do you want to be when you grow up?

Clapping and Crying
with All the Other Moms

I always weep at endings.

The end of the school year slays me every time.

More than any other ending, it marks time for me. The slash on the calendar is dark blood red. This ending has been earned. Yet I don't want it.

The door closing feels heavy and even though I know I have no power to stop it, I feel like running toward it, asking nicely if it could take its time, close slowly, tenderly, and give us a few more days.

The slamming seems final. And it is.

Another year of lunches and rides and notes and homework...the cycles of sports and choir and band and art...the friends that hurt and the friends that helped us heal...the joy of newness and the scary stuff...the failing and fumbling and the tears.

All the laughing and running and playing are dying down over here.

No more Barbie Jeep, and no more sparkly streamers hanging from handlebars. No one wants to play on the slip-and-slide. I remember days of baby pools and strollers and swing sets... the messiness...the laughter...the *living*.

Star Wars figures have taken their place on the shelf, dusty and alone.

I'm wandering around the house trying to look busy (To whom? I don't know. The busy police?) Trying to be busy to take my mind off the ending. But I just wander, not understanding how I feel.

I look at the bookshelf—a safe place to get lost for a while. The books mark our journeys from Junie B. Jones to John Green and I can't seem to part with any. It's like a living scrapbook of words that have fed our souls and kept us company. We will never have too many books. They are our friends, constant and reliable.

I just saw a friend who is moving in a week. She welcomed us when we moved into the neighborhood eleven years ago. We've consumed many cups of coffee and glasses of wine while the kids played, and the years passed. I love her. She was boxing up things and I was in her empty house, and I just couldn't take it. We both just stood there and cried. No words.

Another ending.

I always weep at endings.

The last of my kids will finish up at elementary school this year. The adorable, loving, little, everyone-knows-your-name elementary school. The place where they have taught and nurtured and loved my kids for eleven years. Talk about the end of an era.

We "Clap out" our kids at the end of school. All the parents line up and clap while the 5th graders march out. I think they should call it the "Cry out" for me. I'm anticipating weeping at that ending too. Hey! We should call it "The Clap and Cry Out." Clapping and crying at the same time pretty much sums up motherhood.

Weeping seems bad, right? Like I'm unhappy. But I'm not. I swear.

I'm just confused.

How did I go from eagerly anticipating my first baby to having three kids out of grade school and two in high school?!

How did I go from spoon-feeding peas to worrying about drinking and driving and dating?

My son said the other day that he "hates change." He said, "Change is bad."

Oh, no! I thought. I have to help him see change in a positive light. Change is the only thing we know for sure will happen. We have to get used to it. We have to accept it. It's not bad, right?

Maybe he thinks it's bad because I'm over here crying while looking at baby pictures. What have I done?

I specifically remember my mom talking to me about this. Many times. It's an ending, sure, but it's a beginning too...or it's a beginning and it's exciting and you are happy, but the reason you are crying is because it's an ending too. How many times over the years are we in that space, that in between, the ending and the beginning?

The sadness and the excitement, the saying good-bye and saying hello. It doesn't even matter how many times; I always weep at endings.

I remember once I was crying on the phone to my mom during the college years. I was distraught, things were changing, I just had a break-up, and I was down. This is what she said to me, no joke, and it worked: "Honey, seriously, stop crying. Wash your face, put on some lipstick, get a Diet Coke, and *get out there.*"

Diet Coke and lipstick...the cure-all.

And now I'm the mom. I have to buck up and give the advice now.

I'm not so sure about lipstick. Do we really need that?

And telling them to have a Diet Coke seems archaic, like I didn't get the memo. So do I say, "Have an organic green smoothie?" That doesn't have the same ring to it.

How about this?

Change is part of life. It's difficult, and it's okay to cry. When we cry, we know we are most alive because our heart is feeling things. When we are sad to move on, it means we have loved where we have been, and that is a gift. A treasure. You are building your story, and God is moving you along as you become who you are meant to be. You take all of this with you. All the memories, the people, the experiences, the feelings, the knowledge, the wisdom. You're like a sponge and you absorb it all.

Things are changing, yes, and so are you—you are ready. Be grateful. Take a minute. Let the grateful tears fall...acknowledge that you are a little scared of something new...recognize that you were comfortable and that felt good.

But part of life is getting comfortable with being uncomfortable. Learning that you can do hard things. Trusting that all will be well. It's time to move on now. You do not go alone. Dad and I are with you every step of the way. And God is with you. He knows what you need, and *He can't wait to give it to you.* Life is amazingly beautiful. *Get out there.*

Step joyfully into this new adventure.

I will be stepping out with you...clapping (and maybe even crying) all the way.

 ＊ How do you feel about endings?

 ＊ What have you learned about how to transition into something new?

 ＊ When have you been simultaneously happy and sad?

Letter to My Daughter on Her First Day of High School

I woke up this morning thinking, "Where did the time go?"

I remember the day you were born. Well, actually, I'll be honest—it's a blur. After being induced and then going through twenty-four hours of labor, I was exhausted. And then upon seeing you, I was exhilarated... and scared...and overwhelmed. I felt a keen sense of "everything is different now." I felt blessed and terrified.

I realize now, that's what parenting feels like. You alternate between feeling blessed and terrified.

And on your first day of high school, that describes my emotional state.

First, I want to thank you. You have taught me so much. I am certain now that God uses children to shape and form and teach us. You have taught me, and you continue to do so. I am humbled and honored to be your mom.

As you enter those halls filled with thousands of other high schoolers, there are some things I want you to know. Since you act mortified when I try to sit you down to "talk," I figured I'd write instead, and you can read it when you want to. Plus, I don't have time to put you in the car and drive around which seems to be the only place we can have a meaningful conversation.

Here's what I want you to know.

Some days will be fun and exciting and days that will stink. And this is okay. It is all part of growing up and becoming who you are meant to be. We cannot enjoy the mountaintop without the climb.

If you are going through tough times, remember, there is always hope. There is a rainbow waiting for you at the end of the storm. Always have faith.

Whatever is happening to you matters to me and Dad, and it matters to God. Talk to us. You are never alone.

Sometimes people are nice, and sometimes they are mean. This has nothing to do with you, and everything to do with them. Stay nice.

Boys that are cute on the outside aren't always so cute on the inside. Trust your instincts. Character matters. If you feel something's not right, it's not. Go with your gut.

Drugs are bad. I say it every day, and I know you are rolling your eyes right now but I'm serious. Don't even try them. Say no. Say it again. Say it louder. You are precious and your body and mind and soul will be destroyed by drugs. Don't even start. Don't even try. If you see them in the room, leave. This cannot be emphasized enough. I don't care if you need to blame me and make up outlandish excuses to get out of there—leave, run. On that note, anyone who offers you drugs is not your friend. End of story.

There will be all kinds of people at high school. This will give you a glimpse of what the world feels like. There will be lots of new faces, and you will be tempted to compare yourself to others. Don't do it. Comparison is the tool of the devil. See, the fact is there is no comparison. Each person is unique and beautiful and created by God who loves them. We come in all shapes and sizes. We excel in different things. We have different gifts, but we are all important and vital parts of this world. We were created for a reason, and God has great plans for us. We can't compare ourselves because our journeys are so different. It's like a giant puzzle. We all look different, but without one of us, the big picture would not be complete.

You have to try. You have to try to get good grades, you have to try to make friends, you have to try to get involved, you have to try. You have to put yourself out there to grow. You cannot wait for life to come to you; you have to go out and get it. This can be scary but the more you do it, the easier it gets. Get out there... opportunities await.

Have fun. There is no rush to grow up. Laugh, meet new people, listen, and engage. In every situation, there is some way to eke a little fun out of it...even math class. Life is what you bring to it, so bring joy.

Believe in yourself. This sounds trite but it's true. I believe in you, Dad believes in you, and God believes in you, but what really matters is that you believe in you. When you believe you deserve great things, you will have confidence to go out and get them. When you pray for good things with the expectation that they will happen, God will hear you and answer you.

I've heard it said that we should pray *bold prayers*—that we should not ask for a C; we should ask for an A. So here's my bold prayer for you.

Lord, I ask for great things for my daughter. I do not ask for her to just "get by" and "do okay." I ask that You bless her abundantly. I ask that You give her strength and courage and determination. I ask that You give her eyes to see her own beauty and the beauty in the world around her. I ask that You put her in situations that are positive and life-affirming, and that You give her the right words and the right actions to succeed and to thrive.

I ask for good people in her life—good friends, kind classmates, and inspiring teachers. I ask for teachers that can light a fire in her heart and soul and make her want to shine. I ask for teachers that understand and encourage and inspire.

Be with her. Give her signs to know You are with her. Burrow deep into her heart so she knows she belongs to You. Protect her. I ask for all these things with the expectation that You will provide. I trust You.

Oh, and Lord, before I end this...thank you. Thank you for the gift of my daughter. Thanks for knowing I need her, and she needs me. Thanks for putting us together.

And while I'm at it, please bless and protect all kids starting high school and all moms. This isn't easy, but it is exciting.

See, we are back to the beginning...blessed and terrified.

* What would you say to someone you love as they are entering high school?
* What advice did you receive as a teenager?
* What would you tell your younger self?

What I Really Want for Mother's Day

Mother's Day has me looking through old photographs and reminiscing. My kids are older now. They aren't thrilled to have their picture taken. I have so many good ones from when they were kids. I love the pictures of them all together, the way they hang on each other, lean into one another, and show up as a team. That's a mother's heart, right? That her kids would support one another and walk together through life.

I was thinking about what I really want for Mother's Day. I think we all really want reassurance that the way we mother and have mothered is good enough. We want a nod from the future telling us it's all going to be okay. We want to know if the kids are all right. Amen?

So, here's my letter to my kids this year about what I really want for Mother's Day. Don't worry about getting me a trinket for Mother's Day. Here is my heart's desire:

I pray that you like yourself. That you feel content in the deepest recesses of your heart. That you know how loved, how wanted, and how cherished you are. That you live fully and love deeply and spill kindness out of your pores. That God's light would wrap you up and keep you warm and propel you to shine. I pray you show up with every ounce of your being. That you love honestly and with integrity and with purpose. That people leave your presence feeling good about themselves. That you have a generous spirit. That you will greet each day as an adventure and an opportunity and that even in the boring and tough days, you will laugh and see it all unfolding as it should.

Will you give me this gift? Are you willing to acknowledge this dream of mine? This longing in my heart? Will you live your life—full, authentic, honest, expectant, and joyous? That's what I want.

I want to know that my mistakes and blunders and outbursts only added flashes of temporary color to the memories but no permanent stain. That in my humanness you witness a redeemed soul, far from perfect but living real...my heart set on being better every day. That you receive life as a gift. Precious but not too much so. That you allow yourself to get dirty and take the tough knocks and come out standing, victorious. I pray you jump in the puddles and dance on the table and laugh with abandon. I pray that you listen intently and stay awake to the world while staying apart from it in your heart, careful not to be snared into foolish traps. I pray you find stillness and contentment and joy. I pray that grace would lead in your language and your actions. That faith will always be your cornerstone, deep abiding trust that all is well.

That is what I want for Mother's Day.

I want you, fully alive and present, for the life that awaits you.

This is your gift to me.

    ✷ If you are a mom, what do you really want?

    ✷ As a daughter or son, what can you give to your mom that will bring her joy?

    ✷ How can you forgive your mom for not being perfect?

The Bathroom Speech

After my kids left for school this morning, I was wandering around aimlessly. I went into the bathroom, and it was a complete mess. There were wet towels on the floor, hair from the hairbrush everywhere, toothpaste dripping in the sink. I started wiping and picking up and cleaning, and I thought, *Really, this is what I'm doing right now?*

It was disgusting, and I was disappointed in my kids for leaving it that way. I had this feeling of defeat. I was thinking, *I've raised a bunch of animals. There is no hope for them. No one will want to be roommates with them or marry them if they live like this. I have failed.*

Then I got defiant. *I'm not going to clean this mess. They will come home from school and be locked in the bathroom cleaning for hours. I've had it. There's a new sheriff in town.*

Then about an hour later when I walked by it again, I couldn't stand it. I had to clean it. I gave in. I am a bigger failure than I thought. I didn't teach them right, and now I can't even stick by the consequences. I stink as a mom.

And to pile on, I had to remind my son who is ten to brush his teeth today, and he tried to trick me by just using mouthwash. Why? Why is that easier? How did I raise a kid who doesn't want to brush his teeth? What is going on here? No girl will ever get near him. He's doomed to a life of loneliness because his mother failed him and didn't teach him to brush his teeth.

So, my kids are messy, stinky, ungrateful, unclean, and tricky people.

This got me thinking. What is the mark of a good mom? What do I want my kids to do/be/create? Do clean bathrooms really matter, or do I just watch too much HGTV?

I have spent this morning thinking of what I will say to them when they return home today after school. I have titled it, "The Bathroom Speech." And I will give the speech in the bathroom. I will make them sit on the filthy floor filled with wet towels for effect. (Just to prove I'm not too soft.)

Here it is:

This whole bathroom thing got me thinking that we need to talk.

As you can see, this bathroom is a pit. I feel it is indicative of your respect for me, each other, this house, and yourselves, and I see we have a problem. You *must* clean up after yourselves. Frankly, this (I'll wave my arm around with a disgusted look on my face) is unacceptable.

If I have not shown you properly how to clean the bathroom, I apologize. (I will be prepared with a cleaning solution and wipes.) Here is how you should clean it. (But I won't actually clean the whole thing because that would be me being soft and them being tricky.) Figure out a way to work together so when you leave for school, it is clean.

I know I tend to focus on things like being a good person, being kind, loving God, doing your best work, being honest, and loving each other. And those things are important. They are still important. However, I want to remind you that you still need to do all those things, *and* you need to clean the bathroom.

Thank you. I love you. Let's not let this happen again.

* What room is the messiest in your house?
* Growing up, did you have chores?
* In what ways have you been disciplined?

The Last First Day

Be still my heart.

This is the Last First Day.

My oldest is a senior in high school. *Lord, hold me.*

It seems impossible, yet it's happening all around me. Kids are growing up.

Last night I went up to my daughter's room to tuck her in. Yes, I still like to tuck her in. That's normal, right? If not, don't tell me. It just so happened that the other kids followed me last night. That's totally normal too, right? Is it also normal that I made her lunch today, and I might have suggested some cute earrings and a ponytail? SHE IS ALMOST EIGHTEEN. You guys...I cannot cut the cord. I cannot stop. Seriously, send help.

So there we were, all three kids and mom, snuggling in her bed, tucking her in. As a mom, I was in heaven. ALL MY BABIES WITH ME. You guys, I could not help it. I started crying and talking about when she was young and how much I love her and all the feelings and thoughts. She smiled and patted me, "It's okay Mom." "I know Mom." "Don't worry, Mom."

We talked about how it's the last of the family years. You know, the ones you look back on and say, "Remember when..." Those memories of all the kids in the house, of all the chaos and the mess and the laughter. I just kept going on and on. I think they were just stunned, staring at me and murmuring, "It's going to be okay, Mom."

Yet, they didn't leave. They didn't run out or tell me I'm lame or look at their phones. They listened. They let me have my moment. And then a miracle happened. They let me pray. For them. For me. For Dad. For all the moms and kids and teachers and all the world. Amen.

Everything is changing.

But not yet

We've got this year.

I keep reminding myself that with endings come new beginnings, and I love new beginnings. I remember so vividly when it was just me and Natalie during the early days when her dad went to work, and the others weren't born yet. Just us. I made mistakes with her. I was lost, confused, and usually clueless, and she stuck with me. She didn't have a choice, of course. Where was she going to go? Plus, she didn't know all mothers didn't cut grapes into quarters because they were afraid of choking, and she didn't know or care if our house was messy or if I was messy. I pushed her in the stroller, I took her to the park, and I read books to her, and we met friends together.

We were figuring it out. I can't help but think she has a different understanding of me, one only the oldest child can have, from the days when it was just us and we were together in that new beginning. She was so trusting. Can you stand it? I mean, aren't you just so *honored* to be in this? I'm in awe of this motherhood thing.

Crying again...gotta go.

Praying for all of you moms who are feeling all the feelings today. Let's vow to treasure the gift of our kids...whenever and however we can for as long as we can.

These are the days we will remember.

* What's a happy memory you have with your siblings or parents?

* How often did you pray together as a family when you were growing up?

* If you are a parent, when is the last time you felt sappy and emotional about your kids?

Letter to My Daughter at College Drop Off

Well, it's here. It's time. You are ready.

But am I?

From day one, you have been my sidekick. My laughing buddy. My dreamer, talker, sharer. You have let me walk with you. You have held my hand and let me hold yours. You have listened to my heart. Heck, you are my heart. Walking around outside of me.

Your beauty goes deep. Inside of you, there is a light that shines with hope and promise and infinite joy. You are destined for more. Explore, seek, find, enjoy. Don't be afraid. And if you are, that's okay—do it afraid and step out in faith. Fear is not your destiny. Don't limit yourself. Be open and stay open. Do what brings you joy. Laugh a lot.

Listen to your gut. When something feels weird or off or gross, trust that feeling and leave. Your intuition won't lie. Trust yourself. You know.

Don't walk around with preconceived notions and judgments; just be in the moment. Listen. Open your heart to new people and things. Keep learning. Stay teachable. There is a path before you and it is filled with opportunity and excitement and possibility. Nothing is too good to be true. Dream big.

Some days might hurt. Some days you will want to crawl under the covers and disappear. It's okay. That's normal. Log off your phone and listen to music or take a walk or read a book. Enter back into yourself, the place of knowing inside of you that will nourish you. Look in the mirror and remember who you are and "whose" you are. It's okay to nap and disengage and even cry. Call me. I understand. It's necessary. Don't expect every day to be happy; that's not realistic. But remember if you are having a bad day, it's just a bad day, not a bad life. Feel it but do not get stuck there. Everything will be new in the morning.

You will miss us. And we will be longing for your voice and your spirit. You will leave a hole here that will be glaring at us every time we sit down to dinner. You matter in our home, in our family. We will feel incomplete without you. And yet, it's time.

For eighteen years, your tears have been my tears, your joys mine too. You have grown and learned and in walking through the pain and joy with you, I have learned too. I have had to grow up and say goodbye to patterns of my own and wounds left over from long ago. There's nothing like looking into your daughter's eyes and seeing your own self, your own journey. When I guided you or prayed with you or gave you advice, I was preaching to the young version of myself. All the things I still need to remember. We have healed each other.

Don't get too caught up in the image you portray. Concentrate on the real you. The inner you, your mind and soul and thought life. Fill your mind with all that is true and good. Nourish your body and take care of yourself. You don't need drugs or alcohol. You don't want to be numb. You want to be awake for every single minute of it. You have one wild and beautiful life; don't miss it. Fill your soul with the Truth. Capital T, the one that supersedes all circumstances and stories we tell ourselves. The truth is you are loved, you are seen, you are known, you are worthy, and God has great plans for you.

We are watching and cheering and filled with overwhelming joy for you. Be a cheerleader for others. Be a light, share hope, believe in yourself and in the world. We have no doubt you might rile things up a bit and that's good. Be you. Create a life you love and live it, deeply, passionately filled with joy and gratitude. You've got this!

Also, call your mom.

* What advice did your parents give you when you left home?
* What pitfalls did you encounter that you were not prepared for?
* Write a letter to someone you love who is setting out on their own for the first time.

Today, I Can Fold His Shirts

I've spent today washing, ironing, and folding his shirts. Normally, this is a task I don't love and frankly, don't do very often. He has done his own laundry for a long time now.

But tomorrow, he goes to college. I want him to have clean shirts, and I want him to look nice. And "We are not slobs," and "First impressions matter" and "Put your best foot forward" and all that.

But mostly, I want to spend time with his stuff. I want to do something for him. My grown man of a son. He's independent and capable and leaving. But today, I can fold his shirts.

I'm all melancholy and dreamy, kind of wafting through his stuff.

I'm thinking about these shirts. Today, they seem like no big deal, "It's just a shirt." A necessity. But one day, someone else might put it on and wear it home. One day someone might smell it or sleep with it to remember him.

All the time, we remember what people were wearing. "Remember the guy in the striped shirt?" Or "Right-hand corner, blue shirt..."

I'm thinking about my dad's shirt that I kept in my closet for years after he was gone. To put on. To remember. It wasn't "just a shirt."

I'm thinking how all these shirts will probably be wrinkled from now on. But he will at least do laundry, and he'll use the detergent we bought at Target yesterday and he will smell good. Maybe, getting dressed for class, he will pick one of these up in the coming days and think of home. I hope it makes him feel safe. Comfortable.

I'm thinking about the button-downs that he's packing just in case and the golf shirts for certain events, knowing it's the T-shirts...the old worn-in ones that he will reach for most. Like all of us, we have our outside gear and our inside gear. He's cozy. A hugger. Comfy. Not fussy. Real. He's a T-shirt guy.

I'm thinking about some shirts I've kept for twenty years that I reach for, usually to sleep in. For that time of day we are most ourselves. The times we are most "at home."

I'm thinking of all the T-shirts I've put on over the years. All the teams and the friends and the sorority parties and the boyfriends. All the logos and colleges. I'm imagining all the moms of all the other boys, folding and packing shirts for them. The boys I met along the way. The boys my daughters know. I'm picturing those moms, dreamily wandering through their homes, wondering,

Did I tell him enough? Did I love him enough? Does he know how to be out there in the world without me? Does he know how to be kind? Does he know how to iron a shirt? Even when we know all the answers are yes. We still think, *Should I have loved more? Could I have poured more into him?*

He's my only boy and my youngest, so this is especially bittersweet for me. But it's always a struggle. To hold on, to let go.

To pack them up and move them out. To remember folding the 3T as you're packing the XL.

I'm remembering the little boy now. In his Thomas the Tank Engine T-shirt and his White Sox cap. Elmo backpack. Waiting for the bus. So excited for school. So excited to learn. Ready to go.

He's ready now too. His shirts are ready. It's time.

I did, however, hold back a shirt or two of his. I need some new pajamas.

* What is an ordinary object that holds special meaning for you?

* What do you do on a regular basis that you can bring more intention to?

* What do you do in times of transition to keep calm and feel peace?

There's Nothing to Eat

They come home and go straight to the refrigerator. What sight is more common than a college student just staring blankly into the fridge? And then saying, "We have nothing to eat"?

My kids don't want to make anything. Slapping some bread together with some meat and cheese takes Herculean effort. So, saying we have nothing to eat means, "There is nothing made for me and readily accessible for me to bite into right now."

But I wonder if this is a metaphor for something bigger. Our grown kids, standing on the precipice of adulthood. One foot hurrying to get in and the other sheepishly staying behind the line. Not willing to be done with childhood yet.

They come home for nourishment. Not the kind that fills their bellies but the kind that fills their souls. They want stability, wisdom, and comfort. They want the loyalty of family, the steadfastness of home, the unconditional love that parents offer.

Out there, they are one of many. But here, in here, at home, they are precious, adored, and beloved. They are seen and known and wanted. They don't have to clamor for us to look at them; we can't take our eyes off them. They don't have to feel awkward or scared or unsure. Not here.

Home is where they can be real and rest. I don't think they know how much we love to see their backsides poking out of the refrigerator, their laundry piled up in the front hall, or their car parked without a care in the driveway, out of gas.

I don't think they know. How could they? How could they possibly know the way they look to us?

They may show up messy and disheveled and hungry...body, mind, and soul. Ravenous even. Empty, exhausted, confused. Maybe they've messed up. Maybe they've failed. Maybe they are anxious or depressed. There are times they enter in *heavy,* carrying a load of emotions.

And what do we see? We see the baby God blessed us with and the toddler we cuddled and the school-aged child we laughed with and the student and the athlete and the artist and the musician and the reader and the chess player and the friend. We hear the laughter and see the memories. We remember the prayers and the struggles and the relief. We see light and hope and possibility. We see the person God created.

And we get a glimpse into the way God sees us. He doesn't care how we show up. He's just glad when we do.

* What does home mean for you?
* Where do you go to find comfort?
* How do you believe God sees you?

I Got Kicked Out
of Ballet

I got kicked out of ballet when I was six. My best friend and I were "too silly, "and we talked too much. This is not a surprise to anyone who knows us. My mom laughs about it now, but I wonder if she was embarrassed at the time.

My daughter was in ballet, and all I know for sure is the "ballet bun" is no joke. There was a lot of pressure to get the bun right. They were pulled so tight! But all the little ballerinas were so cute. Ballet didn't stick for us. Turns out dance wasn't her thing.

My other daughter played soccer, and by that, I mean she picked dandelions as she sat down on the field during the game. But she looked so cute in the uniform. I love looking at those photos. Turns out she liked art and music better than sports.

I've pushed and performed and put the costumes on my kids. I've gritted my teeth and felt embarrassed and disappointed when they didn't "dance." But they're not monkeys, for God's sake.

And neither are you. Put the dress on or don't. Play ball or pick dandelions. Dance or be silly or stand against the wall looking bored. Heck, pick your nose in the school play if you want!

While earthly parents will be human and want you to perform, God won't. He delights in you. His eyes twinkle when He sees you.

You light up His room. He loves you just the way you are. He even loved me when I got kicked out of ballet.

And He gets so much joy from your kids. Today. Not when they make the team or get the scholarship or nail the audition. Now. We can learn from our Daddy in heaven.

Gosh, how I wish I could go back to those days when the kids were young. I wish I could just tell their little, beautiful baby selves that it's okay to stand still when the lights are on and people are dancing. And it's okay to dance when the curtain goes down. Either way, you are so loved and adored and cherished.

* What have you tried that was ultimately not for you?
* What activities do you love to do?
* Who are you expecting to perform to make you happy?

Just Be You

Just be you.

That's the advice my friend used to give me when I would go off on a tangent trying to fix myself and figure out my calling, and when I wonder about why I was here and what I should do and what other people think of me.

I used to think he was just trying to get me to stop talking, but now I realize it is good advice.

This came up again today when I was sharing a story with some friends.

On vacation, I was walking the beach collecting shells with my sixteen-year-old daughter. This is totally her thing. She loves to be in Nature, walking slowly, not talking. It's a stretch for me, especially the no-talking part. But honestly, just the fact that she allowed me to walk alongside her is enough for me. I'm desperate to spend time with her and get to know her. As for her, she's not that into me. So we walked in silence.

She picks up everything that is beautiful. Which means she picks up every shell. She doesn't care if they are broken. She has a bucket full of broken shells.

Meanwhile, I'm running some weird imaginary race down the beach looking for perfect shells that are shiny and not broken. I present them to her like it's a contest. Look at my shells, aren't they pretty? I did good, right? Accept me, admire me, love me...

tell me I'm good at this. She just shrugs and continues on her peaceful journey.

At the end of the walk, she has a beautiful bucket of broken, messy shells, and I have one or two lone "perfect" shells.

I could write volumes about what this means. About how obviously she understands life and I don't. How she's having fun in a community of broken shells while I'm lonely with the shells that just want to look like they have it all together. I could beat myself up about my striving and needing attention and wanting to be liked and admired.

But let's wait on that. It gets worse for me.

I say to her, "Why don't we buy some frames or something to put the shells on to make them *useful*?" And she says, "Or we could just let them be."

Or we could just let them be.

It was such an important moment for me as a mom. I saw me. And I saw her. And I started regretting all the times I didn't let her be. I started thinking about all the times I tried to fix everything for her and how I still continue to do it today and how I hope she knows she doesn't need fixing. About how I hope she doesn't resent me and how I wish I could take back all the times I may have given her the impression that she's not enough.

I was telling a few friends about this and about how awful I am as a mother and person, and they stopped me cold.

They reminded me there is no one right way to be and there is beauty in the way my daughter is, but there is beauty in me...

so much beauty. There is beauty in the mother lion me that comes out when my kids need me to defend them. There is beauty in the striving and the fixing when I need to kick it into high gear. There is beauty in my relationships that are messy and complicated. There is beauty in who I am. Even when I screw up and my kids have to teach me. There is beauty in them teaching me.

My friends were saying, "Just be you."

Sometimes I get so caught up in wanting to be better that I forget I'm already good.

I've been asking God lately for direction and He has answered loudly and clearly with one directive: Rest. Stop doing. Don't try to fix or change anything. He wants me to be still and trust that I am enough...that He is enough...that He has me and my daughter in His hands. He's got this.

"In quietness and in trust shall be your strength."
(Isaiah 30:15 ESV)

Here's the thing. God loves me all the time. He wants me as I am. He's saying come to me, let me have your heart...the one that is messy and broken and imperfect...the one that is beautiful and kind and loving and faithful. The one the world needs.

"Just be you," He says. "I'll handle everything else."

* When do you feel most like you?
* When is it difficult for you to "just be you"?
* What is God teaching you through your children?

Watch Me!

We have been at the pool a lot lately. My son loves to go off the diving boards. He spends hours alternating between the low dive and the high dive. Each time he gets on the board, he looks over to me and gives me the thumbs up. When I give him the thumbs up, he'll proceed. If I'm not watching, he will wait or yell, "Hey, Mom, are you watching?" This is why I haven't been reading much this summer. I carry my big book to the pool, but I've been on the same page for weeks.

My son's longing to have me watch him is similar to the way we all want to be seen. How cool to have someone always watching and cheering you on. Wouldn't it be great if before we took a leap in life, we could look over to God and have Him give us the thumbs up? We all want reassurance that what we are doing is right and good for us.

I was in a seminar once and the speaker said her mom hung a picture of Jesus in every room to remind her that He was always watching her. She claims her mom did this to scare her. She said it like, "He's *always* watching..." As in, "Don't try to get away with anything because even if I don't see you, Jesus sees everything." This woman was really traumatized by this and felt very afraid of Jesus. She said she couldn't accept the Eucharist as a child because she was so afraid of Jesus. She was taught that He was a judgmental, punishing God. She was taught to fear.

How different would that message have been if she was told this: Jesus is always watching you. He is everywhere you are, and He loves you so much. He can't take His eyes off of you. He is cheering for you, He is giving you the thumbs up, He is with you always. He is your protection, your comfort, your assurance. He is your friend.

Much better, eh?

It's all in our perspective. It's all in the way we look at it.

As a parent, I know how important it is for my kids to see me there, on the side of the pool, paying attention, giving the thumbs up, clapping, congratulating, and cheering. I realize they are building their perceptions of life based on what they are experiencing.

The diving board is really a metaphor for life. When we are going to take a "leap" in life, what has our experience shown us?

Am I being encouraged? Are people rooting for me? Am I good enough? Am I brave enough? Am I supported?

What has your experience shown you? Are you going to jump off that board or not?

* When have you taken a leap in life?
* Who has been a cheerleader for you in your life?
* Is there something you are considering doing now that feels like a leap of faith?

OFFERING MYSELF GRACE

Lord, thank you for teaching me about myself and the world. I trust You orchestrate it all, and nothing is wasted. As we write about our personal lessons learned, help us look back with compassion for our younger selves. Thank you for the way You designed us and called us and have led us so far. We still have a lot to learn, but we've come a long way.

I was lying there on my yoga mat, exhausted, depleted, desperate. Scripture had been spoken over us as we practiced, sweat mingled with tears, worship music in the background. I was so tired. Tired of pretending and controlling and trying to hold it all together and trying to be everything to everyone.

I was still. Final resting pose. I heard Your voice. "You can rest," You said. I wept. I knew it was You because it was so soft, so kind, so reassuring, pure comfort. And in that moment of my surrender, You brought several women around me to pray. My eyes were closed, and I couldn't see faces. You gathered just who I needed to cover me in prayer. To seal this moment. To minister to me. I was seen and I was surrounded. Lifted up. Carried. Transformed. In rest and in trust and in surrender, I found Your peace.

"In repentance and rest is your salvation, in quietness and trust is your strength."

(Isaiah 30:15 NIV)

Keep showing us the way, Lord. Amen.

Are You Ready to Be a Beginner?

Every time I've gone out a limb and said yes to something new, it has been a huge blessing.

I remember feeling the nudge to sign up to become a Christian yoga teacher. Yoga had helped me so much with my PTSD and with life in general, I figured I'd like to share it with others. The fact that the training I was looking at was Christian wasn't why I was going. Honestly, I thought, *well, I'll learn what I need to know, and then I can teach however I want to teach.* I'm telling you this because I didn't set out thinking, *Oh, this will be a transformative experience with the Lord.*

My personality likes to just jump into things. Sometimes, to be honest, I don't even think. I'm like a horse at the gate ready to launch. I'll say yes and then figure it out. I think people are wired to either be like me or to be the person who studies and asks a lot of questions and does a lot of research before saying yes.

So I called to do my interview before the training started, and the woman on the phone asked me, "Are you ready to be a beginner?"

Hmmm.

I wasn't sure.

What does this mean?

It means I need to be humble. To be teachable. To show up and listen.

Uh oh. Listening is not my strong suit. And as for being humble, my dad used to say, "There's no conceit in your family; you got it all." So, there's that. I have to say, I am much humbler and a far better listener today because I said yes to this question (not having any idea if I was ready to be a beginner) and yes to the training.

A lot of people need to know they will be good at something before they will even try it. Again, not me. I have no problem making a fool of myself. I am not embarrassed to be embarrassed. I often say, "I'll go first!" So, I said yes and signed up for the training.

At the risk of sounding dramatic, I have to say, God seized my heart on my yoga mat.

This was not the way I saw Him inviting me into deeper communion. On a yoga mat? Barefoot? In the desert?

It was there that He taught me what it means to embody my faith. What it means to live and move and have my being in Him.

Here's the thing: He knows what will draw us in, and He uses it. Friends who love music meet God in lyrics and melody. Friends who love books are overcome with His presence through words. Runners meet Him on the running path and in 10Ks and marathons. Artists commune with God when they are creating. You get the point. He meets us where we are. He invites us to do the thing we love, and then He shows up. It isn't about yoga. It's about Jesus getting creative with the way He would grab ahold of my heart.

When I finished the training, I went back to my Catholic church and asked if I could host a Christian yoga class in the parish center. They said yes, so, with the help of some friends, we started to set up and tell people about it. We would be practicing in one of those big, carpeted rooms with the dividers. We pulled the walls in to make it cozy. I brought candles and music and had Scripture verses ready and prayers written. I was nervous but excited. I felt called. Like I was stepping out in faith and like I was stepping into my original design and purpose.

We made twenty-five flyers for the attendees, hoping to have maybe twenty people attend. As the women started arriving, it got crowded. My friend was helping me greet people, and she had to make more copies of the handout. We started to move the walls to create room for more people. There was a log jam at the sign-in table. We were going to start late. Everyone started to set up their yoga mats, and we realized we had to move the walls again.

We expected twenty women. God brought eighty.

It was exhilarating.

We were like children. Laughing, playing, moving, praying, making new friends, and saying yes to God. I have pictures and we are all linking arms leaning back, opening our hearts to God and each other. It was holy.

Not all these women attended church. I've realized over the years, there are lots of people who will not show up for church, but they will show up for a yoga class in a church. It makes me think of Jesus meeting the fishermen at the water while they were out fishing. *Meet people where they are.*

Sometimes when I'm teaching, I say, "Amen?" like a question. I don't expect everyone to answer me as it's sort of rhetorical. But on that night, people started answering, "Amen!"

Amen sounds a lot like "I'm in!" and it means the same thing really.

What about you? Are you in?

Are you ready to be a beginner?

* When was the last time you did something for the first time?

* Who inspires you to try new things?

* Where has God met you?

Nothing Is Wasted

"Nothing is wasted," she said.

I just looked at her like she was crazy since it seemed so disjointed, this life of mine.

Classes and books and studying...for what? I think sometimes. Yoga, workshops, and working out. The running and the striving and the working to be all things.

I see you, He assures me.

The Bibles, so many, and the studies I can't keep straight, my fingers clumsily looking at the table of contents to see how to get to where all the others already are. Lost again but seeking. Searching. No map for me. The path is hidden, only the next step appears miraculously before the abyss. I think I'm the first until I notice the muddy indentation from the soles (souls?) that preceded me.

Fragments of grace. Pieces of holy. I cling tightly to hope.

He shows me the next step.

I say yes. Not knowing why but trusting that the invitation has been offered by the One who sees the big picture.

All the writers and thinkers and philosophers and musicians... the hours spent talking about ideas and dreams...imagining. College days filled with beer and breadsticks and friends who left home for the first time. All the wondering and wandering.

The people...the anticipatory hello and the sometimes hasty goodbye. Other times the final touch lingering, painful, and difficult to forget. Scars...battle wounds for being real, I guess.

Brennan Manning says, "In love's service only wounded soldiers can serve."

The wounds are not wasted.

Fear and panic born from destiny's appointment with a gunman. A desperate soul in need passing his fear onto me rendering me useless. Paralyzed. Afraid.

Doctors and prayers and the Great Healer leading me to breath.

Breath leading me to life again.

Fear not, He tells me.

Marriage and babies and toddlers and teens all needing their own library to tell their story.

And the dance goes on.

My doubt...His reassurance.

My fear...His freedom.

My sickness...His healing.

My following...His leading.

My trust...His abundance.

Nothing is wasted.

* In what ways has God used a negative experience in your life for good?

* How have you allowed God to lead you?

* Where do you see divine threads when you look back on your life experiences?

Preach

There is much debate in churches over the idea of women preachers. Some say they shouldn't preach. But I ask, "Why can't women preach?" It's got me thinking about preaching.

I remember when I was younger my mom read me a book. It was one of those Golden Books with a sweet girl on the front, I think. I can't remember the details, but I remember there were characters in the book doing different jobs. There was a mailman, a doctor, a nurse, a teacher, etc. The doctor was a woman. That must have been pretty radical for the 70s but it wasn't radical for me. It wasn't radical for my mom. My mom told me I could do anything. My mom preached.

My dad preached too. With his kindness and his belief in me. I saw no difference in the amount of love that could be given from a man or a woman. There was no difference. They loved equally and powerfully.

My mom told me about Jesus and His plans for me. She taught me right from wrong. She modeled kindness. She hugged and laughed a lot too. She welcomed people into our home. Make no mistake, she preached.

As I got older, I had teachers who told me I could do anything, be anything, achieve anything. They encouraged me. They were men *and* women. They preached. They preached about opportunity and possibility and hard work and dedication and taking risks and trying my best and believing in myself. Men and women, they preached.

These people did not need permission. They did not need a degree in encouragement. They did not need a board of directors or a council of decorated clergymen to tell them they were good enough. They knew it. God approved them. God. Not man. And He gave them an assignment. He said, "Go love the people in front of you." And then He put the people in front of them! They heard His voice saying, "Encourage that child," "Show up," "Be an example." They did not wait. They could not wait. It was time.

All we have is this moment. Are you going to wait? For permission to preach? From whom?

In college I knew a sorority sister who preached. She talked about Jesus. She shared His Word and His promises. She encouraged us to get to know Him. It was the early 90s. She was nineteen or twenty and did not yet have a college degree. Age and education have nothing to do with preaching.

My kids preach to me! The other day my oldest daughter laughed at me when I said I'm not a hypocrite. She laughed. I asked her why she was laughing, and she said, "Mom, did you not hear what the preacher said? We are all hypocrites!" BOOM.

That's my girl. Preach!

As an adult, there have been so many! There are women pastors who have made an impact on my life. There are writers and speakers and organizers and women fighting for the victims of sex trafficking. Women are on the front lines wiping tears and fighting for justice. Some are in the courtroom, and some are in the church. Together we preach.

There are too many to name here. Think about the women who have helped you. Think about the moments of grace. Consider the examples in your life and thank them for their obedience. When they were called to be an example, they answered that call. Many of them did it afraid.

I would not be who I am today without these preachers. Whether they ever stand behind a pulpit or speak on a large stage or publish their writings...it does not matter. God gave them gifts and opportunities and they answered with a GREAT BIG YES! Yes, I will love that person. Yes, I will listen. Yes, I will tell them about Jesus. Yes, I will encourage them. Yes, I will be kind. Yes, I will forgive. Yes, I will repent. Yes, I will pray. Yes, I will read Scripture. Yes, I will spend time alone with God. Yes, I will listen for His voice. Yes, I will live in joy. Yes, I will be grateful. Yes, I will open my home and my heart and my life. Yes.

And if you call me to it, Lord, I will preach by writing and on a stage and from a yoga mat. I will get to know You so I can hear Your voice. I will not shrink back. I will not be afraid. You go before me and show me the way. Yes, Lord, I will follow You.

See, God does not speak only in the church. He does not only use priests as conduits for sharing the faith. He does not speak differently to men and women. He is speaking to you and me right now.

Our humanness makes us look to the center stage waiting for direction from someone who is "smarter" or "more important" or "ordained" or "better than us." But God is standing there, in the margins, in the hallway, by the bathroom door, beckoning us.

Preaching looks like helping with homework and making dinner and loving your spouse. Preaching is a hug before school or a ride in the rain. It's a phone call and a text and a Facebook post. It's cheering from the stands and standing at the gravesite and bringing flowers to a friend. Preaching is sharing coffee or wine or chocolate. Preaching is putting down the phone and listening with your eyes. Preaching is holding your tongue and choosing kindness. Preaching is staying home and staying out of trouble. Preaching is standing in the gap for your friend who no longer believes and reaching out to God on her behalf. Preaching is choosing to be different so others see that they can be too. Preaching is honoring commitments for the long haul. Preaching is seeing the good in others and pointing it out to them and everyone else. Preaching is love.

So in answer to the question, "Why can't women preach?" I say, they can and they do and they will.

"Do not quench the spirit." (1 Thessalonians 5:19 ESV)

I was in a Beth Moore study, and she always has a great way of explaining things. She was talking about what happens when someone is on fire with the Holy Spirit and the people around them (or maybe one, big, powerful person) come in like the fireman with the hose and just start spraying to put out that fire. What a shame! People, that is not our job! Let the Holy Spirit work through all people as God sees fit. Guess what? Man does not decide who is promoted to speak God's Word and encourage others. *God decides.*

Now go. Preach.

The world needs you.

* When have you preached?
* When have you felt held back by someone else or by yourself from preaching?
* Who has preached to you in your life?

Lessons from the Honky Tonk

The other night I was at a bar in Texas, a good, ole Honky Tonk, listening to a band. Even though I had never been to that venue before, the atmosphere was all too familiar. The darkness. The loud music. The drunk people. The smoke. I went to the bathroom where there was a pack of women smoking pot. The whole place had a foggy feeling. Like a lost memory.

There was a woman there. I've thought about her a lot since that night. She was right in front of me with a man. He seemed to be her boyfriend, at least for the night. They were kissing and grinding and honestly, it was uncomfortable. I didn't know where to look. She was drinking and dancing and wasn't wearing much. But she caught my eye a few times mid-dance. It was like she was looking for approval. Her man didn't seem all that interested which was surprising to me. She was a beautiful woman on the outside. Long hair, fit body, clear skin, big eyes. But there was something missing. She had that Kardashian look about her—a natural beauty with way too much make-up and a self-consciousness that bordered on awkwardness. She was trying too hard. I felt sorry for her.

For us.

I saw myself in bars in the past. Dancing. On tables, in aisles, on stage. I smelled myself hung over and regretful. I remembered myself, sweaty and foggy and showing off. I was just having fun,

I'd say. What a great night, we would recall. All my friends were in the same boat. My throat was scratchy and Sunday was ruined. But we had fun, right? What's the big deal?

When the hymn says, "I was blind but now I see," I think of Romans 12:2.

> "Do not conform to the pattern of this world, but be transformed by the renewing of your mind. Then you will be able to test and approve what God's will is— his good, pleasing and perfect will."
>
> (Romans 12:2 NIV)

I was just doing what everyone else was doing. I wasn't too over the top with my partying by comparison. It's our culture, from high school to college, to our twenties, and even into our thirties and forties. This is what everyone around me was doing. I wasn't a bad person. And neither is she.

We are not disqualified.

I'm so glad Jesus enters right into the debauchery. He is not surprised by us. He is not offended. He sees what's going on, loves us in it, and calls us out of it and into more. He begins the work of transformation if we let Him.

So much of Christianity is whitewashed clean. We go to church wearing our Sunday best and we volunteer and we do what's expected of us, pretending we were always this way. People on the outside look in and think they could never belong. They aren't cleaned up and spit-shined enough. I dread the thought of all the pretending of churchgoers keeping others away from Jesus.

Here's the thing: If Jesus came for anybody, He came for that woman in the bar. So eager to be seen. So desperate to be known. So hungry for approval.

I recognized her because she was me. I can't forget her. And I'm sure beyond a shadow of a doubt, Jesus hasn't forgotten her either.

* What do you see clearly now that you did not understand when you were younger?

* How can you offer yourself grace as you look back at your younger years?

* How can you show grace and love to those around you?

This Year I Will Wear Jeans That Fit

I was trying on jeans the other day. I found a box with a bunch from years past, and I tried them all on. Every brand was in there. And every size. All the styles...skinny, flared, boot cut, boyfriend, ripped, cropped, light, dark, stretchy, bedazzled, high-waisted mom jeans. Oh, and low-waisted. So low-waisted. Why?

Now I see they represent all the different phases of my life. There is the young stage, the mom stage, and all the sizes up and down during the pregnancy years. The fancy going-out jeans, the run- around-town jeans, the ones you wear with your boots, and the ones that can handle heels. Some have been tailored to fit like a glove, others hang low, hand-me-downs from my husband, ripped and torn and way too roomy. Some have paint splats from my days of painting furniture. Some are ripped on purpose, others from wear.

Funny note: When I was a teenager, my mom took me to the mall. She succumbed to my begging and pleading and bought me a pair of Guess jeans. They were ripped. I had to have them! We came home and I was so excited to show my dad. Now let me give you some background. My dad was born in 1925, lived in poverty as a kid, was a Marine in WWII, and went to college on the GI Bill. So you may know where this is going.

He looked at me and said, "I don't understand why you would buy ripped jeans. They are new! If you want ripped jeans, I'll take you over to Farm and Fleet and buy you some jeans for $9.99 and I'll rip them for you!" He wasn't mad. He was sincerely confused. Incredulous even. It wasn't the first or last time I left him speechless.

There was always something I just "had to have." Forenza sweaters anyone?

As far as jeans go, there is no other item of clothing that I love more. Jeans are my jam. I once had a photographer come over to my house to take photos for my website. I had a lot of different outfits. But the minute I put on jeans, cowboy boots, and a crisp white blouse, the mood changed. I was comfortable and free! I feel like I'm myself in jeans. However, I've realized that more times than I care to admit, I have worn jeans that make me feel "not myself." I'm embarrassed to say there were times when I held my breath, lying on the bed to zip my jeans, spending the evening feeling like a stuffed sausage, not being able to bend over. I cringe at the memory of this.

After trying on all these jeans the other day, I realized I'm ready to move on.

I'm not saying I won't keep them. I will pack them away in a box to pull out when I feel like reminiscing. I will think of them like a living, fashion photo album. Hopefully, there are no actual pictures of me in the low-rise jeans going full plumber. I mean, what were we thinking? When our jeans require special underwear or force us to go commando, maybe we need to be rethinking our choices. Hindsight is 20/20. Hindsight. Get it?

I'm all about comfort now.

I have grown up. I am wiser and a little wider. And it's okay if some of my old jeans no longer fit. There are other things in my life that no longer fit. It's part of growing up.

In the new year, I will wear jeans that fit. I'll wear them like a boss with my boots and my big, blingy Texas belt buckle. I'll wear jeans that make me feel like me. The real me. The age I am now. The me that understands where she has been and is joyfully expectant about where she is going. The me that has mothered three children into adulthood. The me that knows I don't have to fit into a size six to be beautiful. Also, no one cares. There are many more pressing issues.

At this stage of life, I now humbly understand how small I am (even if my butt isn't). I'm embracing my whole self—flaws, mistakes, successes, all of it. I own it all. I love me.

I have earned this confidence.

You have too. You've earned the right to shine in whatever fits you. Whatever makes you feel good.

Let's do this. Let's strut together out into the world. Confident and courageous. Bold and strong. Let's show our daughters what aging comfortably really looks like. I can see it now, and it's beautiful.

A big band of women, walking together arm-in-arm, worthy and beloved, comfortable in their skin...and their jeans.

* What is your relationship to jeans?
* What outfit do you feel most beautiful in?
* What does it mean to you to be comfortable in your skin?

Courage to Commit

I went to a wedding last weekend. I love weddings! Every time I hear wedding vows, I get tears in my eyes. The words are so beautiful.

Imagine...we stand up and say yes to a lifetime commitment to love. We promise unconditional love to another person. As imperfect people, this is a leap of faith. This kind of commitment takes courage.

The priest at the wedding this weekend said, "We have no idea what people, events, and circumstances will define this union." Isn't that true? We cannot predict what will happen, but we are hopeful, expectant, and full of faith. We don't know what our story will be and that's the beauty of it. That's the romance. The two of us against the world!

At the wedding, I sat next to a couple that was talking about having a baby. They were wondering...should they, shouldn't they, how will their lives change? I have found that if we think about things too much, we all become hesitant, fearful, and unsure.

In a host of circumstances—marriage, parenting, careers—we can get too much in our heads. I'm not recommending we throw caution to the wind and live life without thinking. But I know that if I think too much about something, I can have "paralysis from over analysis."

I found a quote on a Starbucks cup (inspiration is everywhere!) that speaks to this. The quote is not attributed to anyone but this person sure was wise.

> *"The irony of commitment is that it's deeply liberating—in work, in play, in love. The act frees you from the tyranny of your internal critic, from the fear that likes to dress itself up and parade around as rational hesitation. To commit is to remove your head as the barrier to your life."*

Don't you love this? We do dress up our fear, don't we? We call ourselves "realistic" or "cautious" or "practical" when often we are just plain scared. Sometimes we need to say yes first and then figure out how to make it all work.

Our head is often a barrier to our lives. Our little mind tells us to hesitate and fear. But if we listen to our heart, well, that's a different story.

* ✳ When have you listened to your heart to make a big decision?
* ✳ When were you fearful and said no to something you wanted to do?
* ✳ What big leap of faith has paid off for you?

Amazing Grace

God is everywhere. He is in a sunset, a baby's laugh, a cup of coffee with a friend, a kiss from your first grader, a hug from your husband or wife. He's in church, He's on the beach, He's with you walking the dog, He's at work. You may feel His presence, or you may not. Just because you don't know He's there or you don't believe He's there, doesn't change the fact that He is there.

I went to a conference once and I heard a woman talk about God. She said she found a lump and went in for a biopsy and then had to wait for the doctor to call her to tell her if she had cancer. She said she kept telling herself, *whether you get the news you hope for or the news you dread, God's grace is the same.* Then she repeated that same quote about three more times. This was about ten years ago, and I have never forgotten it.

She said it with such conviction. You could have heard a pin drop in the large arena filled with thousands of people. I imagine everyone else was doing what I was doing, wondering if they could really believe those words if they were waiting for that same phone call.

I've thought of these words of wisdom many times since then. I've thought of them when I've gotten bad news. I've thought of them when I've been waiting for the phone to ring. I've thought of them when my friends have gotten bad news. I've thought of them when people I love have died. What I now realize is that even when I have changed, God has not.

And now I believe...

On a good and sunny day, when all is well with the ones you love, God's grace is the same.

When there is uncertainty in life, God's grace is the same.

When all your kids are safe and happy and healthy, God's grace is the same.

When the world is literally turned upside down and the fear is debilitating, God's grace is the same.

When there's good news of a new baby, graduation, promotion, God's grace is the same.

When the night is dark and your heart is heavy with worry and doubt, God's grace is the same.

When I've made a mistake and I need to be forgiven, God's grace is the same.

When someone I love has died, God's grace is the same.

Whether you get the news you hoped for, or the news you dread, God's grace is the same.

* When have you experienced God's grace in a difficult time?
* What would you say to a loved one experiencing challenges?
* What truth helps you stay grounded and peaceful?

What?
Is That Weird?

I have Dr. Seuss and Proverbs quotes on little signs sitting on my windowsill.

For those of you who know me, this is not a surprise.

I'm a *both/and* person.

I love to read Scripture and I love to read Dr. Seuss. Also, Winnie the Pooh is full of wisdom.

I love Jesus and music, movies, TV shows, magazines. Red carpet fashion is my favorite.

Years ago, my daughter told me, "It's kind of funny mom, I mean, you love Jesus so much and you read the Bible and stuff, but you just posted something about Justin Timberlake."

To that, I respond, "What? That's weird?"

I think many of us are afraid of putting our faith in Jesus in the middle of our lives. We put our Christianity in a box. It's over there. We take it out on Sunday. It has nothing to do with this party I'm going to or me binging a new show on Netflix.

Many of us have two separate people in us: the one that goes to church and talks about prayer and Scripture and Jesus and the other one. The one who loves pop culture and having fun and keeps up on the latest movies and music. The heathen.

I was just kidding about the heathen thing. I don't think these things are mutually exclusive. God is creative, and I believe He wants us to enjoy art and music and food and cultural things. Everything? No. But I'm certain He doesn't want His children walking around, clutching our pearls, screaming about how awful everything is. If you don't like it, don't read it or watch it. He has given you the gift of discernment. Use it. But someone else may not have the same conviction as you about something.

Let's not "should" all over each other.

There is freedom in Christ.

God created each of us and knows us intimately. When He calls us individually, He tailors His call to our original design. I'm not surprised I have received conviction and inspiration and encouragement through movies and music. The sovereign Creator of the universe is calling the shots, directing the film, writing the story, and He will use it all to bring us closer to Him.

Inspiration is everywhere. What a beautiful, creative, energizing world we live in. Don't miss it!

✳ Are you a both/and person?

✳ Where do you find inspiration?

✳ In what ways might someone say you are a contradiction?

Wear the Boots!

I was looking at a photo of me on stage speaking at an event. I was sharing a breathing meditation with Scripture, worship music, and some light chair yoga. I was wearing cowboy boots. When I saw the photo, I started crying.

I was so grateful for the opportunity to share with this group of women. I shared my testimony about suffering from panic and anxiety after being held up at gunpoint. I was able to tell them the body really does keep the score and God uses our bodies to send us signals. I also had a chance to share how God entered in so He could integrate me, body, mind, and soul. To find myself twenty-four years later, sharing this story of redemption and freedom. It took my breath away right there on the stage. And again, when I saw the photo.

You know when you get in the flow and let the Spirit lead? When you take your head out of it, and you speak from the heart? That's what I did. I don't remember the photo being taken, and I don't remember what I said, to be honest. It wasn't what I had meticulously written and rewritten the weeks, days, and nights before. It wasn't what I thought I "should" say or what I had "practiced." It was what God wanted me to say.

A wise friend once told me, we prepare with our heads, but we lead with our hearts. There comes a time to put down the paper and just feel it. He has been working on me as I write and speak more, and He is showing me that I can't worry about how my words are received. For one, I have no idea what the audience is thinking. Whether it's one person or 10 or 100 or 1000. I have no idea how they will perceive me. What I do know is that God has called me to share my story. In obedience, I share.

Have you ever had God tell you to say something to someone and when you do, it's not received well? The person doesn't react the way you want them to. God has revealed to me that that is an issue with me. If the posture of my heart is to be obedient to the Lord, then all I can do is follow where He leads me. How people react to that is none of my business. I can have no expectation of the response. Sure, accolades and high fives and "atta girls" are amazing. "Likes" on Instagram and Facebook, books sold, rooms filled, are all exciting. But that can't be our "why" because then what happens when all that stops?

When I was getting ready for this event, I had my boots on, and I looked in the mirror and heard a voice saying, "Don't wear those boots. They are too much. Don't be too much. Blend in. Wear tennis shoes, or something less blingy." (My boots have studded crosses on them!)

But then I heard God say, "Wear what makes you come alive. Wear what you love. Show up as you. You are not too much. Bring it all." So I wore boots. And I told the young women in the audience that the enemy will try to tell them that they are too much or not enough. I told them that we can spend our whole lives "shoulding" all over ourselves. I showed them, with my boots, that we can show up as ourselves! In fact, it's the only way. God calls you *as you*. Don't miss your own life. Don't hide.

I showed the photograph to a friend, and I said, "Isn't this beautiful?"

My friend said, "Oh, yes, that right there is a friend of Jesus."

Turns out for me, that's the only "atta girl" that really matters.

* What do you wear that makes you feel strong and bold?
* What voices do you hear that you have to shush and overcome?
* What story is God asking you to share?

Thank You Letter to My Body

Body, thank you for being there for me.

Thanks for getting me up that rope in gym class in middle school, and thank you for all of those glorious bike rides down the big hill in our neighborhood on the way to the pool every day in the summers. Thank you for the way you have carried me in the water on skis and rafts and just plain old swimming. I love the way you can jump on a trampoline, and, oh gosh, thank you so much for the skiing and the climbing and all the fun stuff you carry me to do in the mountains.

Thanks for all of the walks to and from school and the subway and the bus and all over campuses, the one I attended and the ones my kids went to. Thank you for carrying me and allowing me the joy of birthing and holding my babies. Thanks for my babies.

Thanks for the years of running and yoga. The bending and stretching and breathing. Yes, thank you for the breath. And thank you for the way you hug, and the way you love and the way you sense the world around us. Thank you for the belly laughs and the butterflies and the goosebumps. Thank you for sending warning signs when I'm not well. Thank you for recovering.

I'm sorry for the abuse, physical and emotional...I'm sorry about the fried food and the beer and the wine and *all that chocolate*.

I'm sorry for overindulging so many times. Thank you for hanging in there. Oh gosh, sorry about the sun—I regret the iodine and baby oil and tin foil. Sorry about the blisters.

At times I have taken you for granted and criticized and been downright unappreciative. I'm sorry for the words I said to you and about you that were not kind. But no more. I will honor you.

Same goes for my hands. Thanks for the years of shaking and reaching and holding. Thanks for the ability to touch and feel and pray. Thanks for the clapping and snapping and pointing and waving. Thank you for all the hellos and all the goodbyes.

Lord, give me eyes to see the wonder and beauty of my body. The way You knit us together is miraculous. Give me a heart full of gratitude for the way You designed us.

Help me to remember that years and experience only enhance beauty. That the joy I seek often comes with wrinkles from laughing and sunspots from enjoying the world and a few extra pounds from lingering dinners with friends. Joy on the inside makes you glow on the outside. Help me to teach my kids about that kind of beauty. Help me to model that kind of beauty, the glowing from the inside out kind. The kind that never fades.

* Look at a picture of yourself and speak words of love and affirmation to the person you see in that picture.
* What would you like to apologize to your body for?
* How are you feeling about growing older?

I've Made it Through Everything So Far

You know how you look back at some things and cringe about the way you behaved at that point? (Maybe you don't but I have more than a few examples of cringeworthy behavior.) I've accepted that to get me where I am today, I needed to have each and every experience I've had. Every embarrassing experience, every nervous moment, every breakup, every friendship, every job played a vital role in getting me here today. One little thing changes, and the whole thing is different.

Take a minute to think of your most embarrassing moment. (If you are me right now, you're thinking, *Which one?)* It's really bad, huh? What did you learn from it?

Now think of your biggest heartbreak. I know, it makes your stomach hurt. Take a moment, I'll wait. What did you learn from that?

Now think about interviewing for jobs in college. Oh sorry, is that up there with your embarrassing moments?

Think about the first day of high school. The seniors sat on the steps and made fun of the freshmen. We were all dressed alike and hovered so close to each other we couldn't move. We felt gangly and awkward. (Just for reference here, Cindy Crawford was a senior in my high school when I was a freshman, so you think *you* felt gangly and awkward?)

Think of what your hair looked like in the 80s.

Think about speech class.

Think about when your best friend decided she hated you. Or maybe everyone just started ignoring you for no reason.

Think about your first job. Think about the first day.

There are many other examples of growing experiences that I could insert here, but, frankly, I'm starting to feel ill. Funny how the same "butterfly in the stomach" feelings can resurface twenty, even thirty years later, huh?

Sort of makes you realize what your (older and wiser) parents were talking about when they said, "That which doesn't kill you will make you stronger."

Don't you feel like a superhero at this point?

* What has made you strong?
* Describe a time you went through something that made you resilient.
* What used to scare you that no longer does?

Sufficient Grace

God's grace is sufficient.

In 2 Corinthians 12:9 we read:

> "But he said to me, 'My grace is sufficient for you, for
> my power is made perfect in weakness.' Therefore I
> will boast all the more gladly about my weaknesses,
> so that Christ's power may rest on me."
>
> (2 Corinthians 12:9 NIV)

As of today, I believe it.

No more striving. No more reaching. No more grasping and clinging and hoarding. No more thinking, *I have to be perfect to measure up.* No more pride.

Well, at least for today. Maybe I should say at least for this hour. I already messed up this morning.

Old habits die hard.

Just this morning I was talking to a friend, and she was telling me she really liked my writing. I was feeling proud and pumped up. Then she mentioned some writers I admire and a possible opportunity to be featured by them and asked me if I have gone to their website. My mind immediately started churning with how I was going to achieve more and get more and be known more and *be somebody.*

I forgot.

I already am somebody.

I am the beloved child of the King. I am fearfully and wonderfully made. I am blessed and I am a blessing.

It doesn't matter what I do. It matters that I'm His.

I matter.

I've heard it said that this is one of the greatest desires of our hearts—to matter. We don't want our lives to go unnoticed.

Maybe in the past this meant that we wanted to serve others, raise healthy children, and speak kind words.

This reminds me of the Emerson quote I have hanging in my house:

> *"To laugh often and much; to win the respect of intelligent people and the affection of children; to earn the appreciation of honest critics and endure the betrayal of false friends; to appreciate beauty; to find the best in others; to leave the world a bit better, whether by a healthy child, a garden patch or a redeemed social condition; to know even one life has breathed easier because you have lived. This is to have succeeded."*

Do we still believe this defines success? Or now does success mean we must have a reality show, write a book that ends up on the *New York Times* bestseller list, be followed by thousands on Twitter, and make millions of dollars while looking perfect?

There have been times that I've fallen into the trap of believing that my worth depends on how the world sees me, so I have transformed myself to the world. This has made me feel uncomfortable and icky in my heart.

This is a gift because those feelings are God's warning signs. That gut feeling that something is "not right" is the Holy Spirit whispering, "Reroute, turn, stop...let's review...where are we going...why?"

We read in Romans 12:2:

> "Do not conform to the pattern of this world, but be transformed by the renewing of your mind. Then you will be able to test and approve what God's will is— his good, pleasing and perfect will."
>
> (Romans 12:2 NIV)

And in *The Message* in Ephesians 2: 2 it says:

> *"You let the world, which doesn't know the first thing about living, tell you how to live."*

I love it when I read the Bible and I get schooled. I will be thinking, *Are you talking to me?* and then I realize without a doubt, *He is talking to me!*

Just in case you aren't sure...Yes, He's talking to you too.

You matter.

* When have you thought your achievements equal your worth?
* Where does your worthiness come from?
* How do you define success?

GRACE MOVES

Lord, thank you for the plot twists in our lives. Thank you for the fork-in-the-road moments. Thank you for going before us in all things and never leaving our side. You are writing a beautiful story with our lives.

Thank you for interrupting us. Thank you for disturbing us. Thank you for inviting us to get out of our comfort zones. As we write about the times You asked us to go, to move, to take action, please remind us of Your provision and protection. We never move alone.

No matter where we are, You are there. From the windy city to the town they insist on keeping weird, You are the same. From the freezing winters to the sweltering summers, You are the same. From "you guys" to "y'all," You are the same.

From the minivan to the truck, You are the same. From football to FOOTBALL, You are the same. From snow boots to cowboy boots, You are the same.

We cling to what we know. We grasp for what we can explain. But You invite us to open our palms to receive. To stop gripping. You beckon us into the new. You make a way. You place people on the path to support us and encourage us.

And You surprise us with tacos and live music and cool lakes and beautiful hiking trails. Because You love us...wherever we are.

Lord, Help us to follow You and trust You. Amen.

He Got the Job

"I got the job." My husband was tentative. Apologetic? Afraid? He had wanted this. He had interviewed and traveled and hoped for this and fought for this. Now that it was here, he wondered, *Do I really want this?* At least that's how it sounded.

But looking back, maybe he was just scared of my reaction, thinking, *Does she want this? Is she really okay with moving our family across the country? Am I making a mistake?*

"I'm happy for you," I said, my stomach on the floor and my head spinning.

"I want you to be happy *for us*," he answered.

Sitting on our bed, I was practicing my deep breathing and praying for the right words. I was silent, which is rare. I had no idea what to say because my mind was moving in waves. He stood there watching me.

We had lived in the same community for fifteen years. And the same state for our whole lives. I had never even been to the place we would now be dragging our three teenagers to. The kids. Uh oh. Panic started setting in.

"I want you to be happy for *us*," he said.

At that moment, he clarified something important for me. *We*, the two of us and our kids, are more important to him than the job.

He wasn't moving, *we* were moving.

The doorbell rang, right at that moment. Somehow, I walked downstairs to open the door, and it was my dear friend. She immediately said, "What's wrong?"

And I told her through tears, "We are moving to Texas."

"It's okay, it's okay, it's okay," she kept saying as I stared into space, shaking on my front stoop.

Later that day, I was wandering aimlessly around the backyard, adrenaline pumping, fear taking over. I had to call work and tell them that I couldn't host a workshop we had planned because I *wouldn't live here anymore.*

As I began to tell my colleague, I started spiraling, I couldn't breathe, I was babbling, and my voice was getting louder. Panic was setting in, my thoughts were racing, *What have we done?* I was pacing back and forth on the driveway.

I told her what's going on, barely getting the words out through my tears, and she said, "Stop. You know none of this is a surprise to God, right?"

It knocked the wind out of me.

And then, I could breathe again.

In slow motion, like a scratching record or a car screeching to a stop, I was slapped awake. "None of this is a surprise to God," she said confidently with faith. And she was right. He is writing my story. I guess it was time for a plot twist.

We were moving to Texas. *He* was already there.

* What has surprised you in your life?
* Write about a plot twist in your own story.
* What truth has someone shared with you that blessed you?

If These Walls Could Talk

If these walls could talk, what would they say?

Would they talk about the love? And the tears? And the growing pains?

Did they see when I was unsure and afraid and stepping out the door with trepidation?

Could they feel when I returned and sank deep into the comfort of home?

Do they know how much I needed this place?

Do they realize how it made me feel to call this home? Proud. Safe. Blessed.

Would they talk about the laughter and the silliness? What about the dancing and the music?

What about books and movies and laughter?

Did you see how the lamplight looked from the street? Did you see it and call it cozy?

Because inside it was. Cozy. Warm. Friendly. Kind.

Peace.

It isn't perfect. But that's good because neither am I. We fit. With all our quirks, we held each other.

It embraced me. It soothed me. It sheltered the people I love.

If these walls could talk, I think they would whisper blessings. I think they would tell me it's okay to go now. It's time.

They would hold my sacred secrets and wish me well.

* What words would you use to describe your home?
* Write about a memory in a previous home.
* What is non-negotiable to you when it comes to creating a home?

Open Doors

"If you are a dreamer come in
If you are a dreamer a wisher a liar
A hoper a pray-er a magic-bean-buyer
If you're a pretender come sit by my fire
For we have some flax golden tales to spin
Come in!
Come in!"

—Shel Silverstein

I have always loved this poem. To me, it is about open doors, new possibilities, welcoming hospitality, community, and encouragement. It says you are enough, you are chosen, you are invited, you are wanted. Come in and share life with me. It's going to be fun.

I know Shel Silverstein is not Jesus, but I can't help but think Jesus might say the same thing. Whoever you are, wherever you've been, come sit with me, let's share stories, let's do life together. Come in!

We moved this past week into our new home. After months of being in temporary housing, it feels good to settle in and unpack.

I love the doors of our new home. I actually love all doors. They hold such possibility.

From both sides.

Maybe you are the one inside, beckoning others to join you... Come in! Come in!

Maybe you are the one on the outside hoping to be invited, filled with curiosity, glimpsing inside, excited about the possibility of new things.

I feel like I'm on both sides right now.

God is opening this new door and saying, Come in! I've got great plans for you. Let's do this.

I am excited. I feel loved and protected. I say yes. I step through the door. Another new door.

I trust.

And then I feel I must do some inviting of my own:

> *Jesus, come into this space and fill it up. Fill us up. Bless each and every corner of this home with Your presence and Your grace. Teach us to be more like You. Laugh with us and be with us as we eat, pray, talk, learn, grow, and love. In our early morning grogginess and our late-night prayers...when the sun sets and rises...in our arguments and disappointments and struggles... in our celebrations and our accomplishments and our dreams coming true.*
>
> *In those moments when we wonder and we doubt and we let fear creep in, be there to remind us and to reassure us and to comfort us. Show us who we are and what we are living for. Come into the messiness and love us. Right now. As we are. We are in-process, and You know it and You love us anyway. We put our faith and trust in You.*

We invite You in.

It is because of You that we can step through new doors with bold confidence and joyful expectation.

You are doing a new thing and we are grateful.

Come in! Come in!

* What doors have you walked through in your life?
* What is God inviting you into right now? Where does God want you to do the inviting?
* How do you define home?

Just Moved

Today was the last meeting of a group I joined when I first moved here. It's called, "Just Moved" and it's for people who, well, just moved. Obviously.

I was thinking about how moving is actually a big thing. There are books about it. It's up there on the list of "stressful life events." They created a group, a ministry, for those of us in this transition. It's not easy.

At the beginning of our time together ten weeks ago, we wrote on a card how we were feeling. Acknowledging that we were feeling *all the things*, including joy and excitement and freedom, we were instructed to write down some things we were struggling with in particular. Today, they gave us back our cards and asked us how we are doing in these areas now, ten weeks later.

The things I was struggling with—expectation, grief, and loss of identity.

Expectation, meaning I was struggling with my own expectations of how my life *should* look, of how our kids' lives should be. I also realized I have expectations about what I'm going to get and how I'm going to be treated and what is going to happen. I expect, and then when I don't get it, I'm disappointed. This is something I'm working on with the Lord, and I believe I have heard clear instruction from Him on this: "Have no expectation. Do not limit what I can do in your life. Trust."

Grief is something I wrote down because I happened to be crying at the time. I would not have said grief on my own, but then we started talking about the different emotions. I started crying, and I thought, *Wow, I'm grieving.* Ten weeks ago, I really missed my people. I still miss them, of course, but now I'm cherishing and not clinging to the things I've had to say goodbye to.

Loss of identity. Yep. I had nothing and no one defining me. I wore no labels. I was free. And guess what? I missed my little boxes.

Like an animal, I felt comfortable in my cage. I was confused when I was free to roam. And like a prisoner, I stood looking at the open road and freedom and I couldn't move.

If I'm not all those things I thought I was. If I'm not all those things I made you think I was. If I'm not all those things you think of me...who am I?

And then, today, in our small group, it hit me like a ton of bricks.

I had to lose my identity. I had to go through that shedding of all the false selves to know who I really am. I wouldn't have done it on my own so *God moved me.*

I've spent more time with God here in Austin than ever before. There have been times when it has been me and Him only. And I have never felt alone.

Our circumstances, locations, relationships, jobs...all of that is fluid and can change. But God...He's steady as a post. He never changes and He travels with us!

So, as to how I'm feeling now—my expectations were getting in the way because I realize now God has better and bigger and more glorious plans than my mind can even imagine.

Grief is gone and is replaced by something else—gratitude. I have been loved so well in my life and I have connected with people that have changed me...that have nurtured me and laughed with me and supported me. This truth is so overwhelming at times all I can do is say thank you.

And the loss of identity. Yes, I lost my identity. The one that was based on what I did, how I looked, who I knew, and where I lived. But I found my real identity. My identity in Christ. His daughter, chosen, beloved, protected. That's the identity I'm going to need moving forward. God knew that. So He moved me.

* Have you ever moved to a new location?

* What is your identity?

* When in your life has something difficult helped you grow?

Show Me Me

My friend taught me to pray this prayer, "God, show me me." When we pray this, we have to be ready, right? I mean, who knows what He will show us? We can be sure that what He reveals, He will heal. So we enter, unafraid.

Right?

Hmmm.

It's scary to be revealed. We spend most of our lives trying to hide. Even in our bravado or our need to be relevant and fabulous. Even when we are "out there" with our bold selves. Even then, it's sorta fake, right? It may not be totally fake, but there are parameters.

We learn what is appropriate to reveal, we learn what society sees as acceptable weakness. We show the world our sometimes false humility as we admit our shortcomings, the ones we know aren't so bad. Then we pat ourselves on the back for being humble.

We stop there because going deeper is not polite and people say or imply, "Keep that stuff to yourself" and "TMI." We look around and think, *This is all just really fake and weird and my mask is starting to hurt.* So we turn to God and ask Him, "What's the deal here?" And He starts to show us...us.

The shallow, fake kind of revealing is not what God does. It's not the kind of unveiling that happens when we ask God...our Creator...the One who knows every hair on our head...the only

One who understands our every thought, need, whim, fault, sin... when we ask Him for revelation, it is *scary*.

And not.

Because He never leaves.

You know how with people, you can ask for truth and then become so defensive, you decide to sever the relationship? It's easier to walk away from the relationship than to face the truth. So we leave. And others leave. Because it's just too messy to stay.

God's not like that.

He stays, waits, reveals, peels the layers back gently, speaks Truth, holds us, loves us, stays in the mess so He can save us from ourselves. He makes the scary safe.

I've heard people say it's like peeling an onion. God doesn't reveal everything to us at once. It would be too much for us to handle. He is gentle. He is full of mercy and grace.

There is so much in the world about self-help. But I'm glad I have Jesus. I don't have to help myself every time. Especially when it feels heavy and dark and deep. I have someone to go to, and He will share my burdens. He will teach me the unforced rhythms of grace. He will call me to repentance and reconciliation and healing. He is the source of peace and joy. I don't have to do this alone. I don't have to fix myself and work harder and run faster and strive more.

> "But he said to me, 'My grace is sufficient for you, for my power is made perfect in weakness.' Therefore I will boast all the more gladly about my weaknesses, so that Christ's power may rest on me. That is why,

for Christ's sake, I delight in weaknesses, in insults,
in hardships, in persecutions, in difficulties. For when I
am weak, then I am strong."

(2 Corinthians 12:9-11 NIV)

He will show me me, and I may be overwhelmed or sad or excited
or fearful or in awe. He can handle all of it. It's a starting point.
It's like He is dropping the pin on Google maps. Here we are
now. And then we are ready to find our way. We walk this road
together.

What a relief.

* What has God shown you about yourself?

* What has been revealed to you that has felt overwhelming?

* When do you most feel God's presence?

Go Ahead— Surprise me

Nothing is a surprise to God.

But He loves to surprise us.

When we moved, I had no idea what to expect, but I often found myself pleasantly surprised. Have you ever felt surprised by God? Sometimes I think He is having fun showing off. I remember once telling a friend about something going on in my family, and it was affecting all of us. I was lamenting that all the kids were being affected. She said the most beautiful thing. She said that if we all take part in the suffering, we can all be a part of the celebration when God gets us through it. Even in our suffering, He surprises us with blessings.

He really was showing off when we moved.

When my daughter came home and said she was joining a Bible study, it was a surprise to me but not to Him.

When my husband met people at work for the first time at his new office in Austin and they told him they had "been praying for him and his family," this was a surprise to my husband because people just don't say stuff like that in Chicago. But God knew. He heard those prayers, and He planned for those words to fall on my husband's surprised but grateful heart.

When I was standing in that church weeping with the worship music, arms raised and heart open, He was not surprised.

When I opened my door and my dog ran out and started playing with the dogs on our sidewalk, I ran out to get him and met my dear, sweet friend right there in front of my house. He was not surprised when we started talking and within minutes were tearing up and hugging.

But that's not all. She is an artist and also lived in the Midwest. She was explaining it to me, and I couldn't even believe it. I had one of her pieces in my home, a sign that says, "Let your light shine." What an amazing surprise. I picture God smiling when we are together, eight years later, laughing and helping each other shine.

With every box unpacked, each rental place (there were two), buying a home, selling a home, meeting new people, new schools, figuring it all out...through every single moment, He is not surprised. He is present and aware. He goes before me and makes a path for me. He protects me and provides for me. He does the same for you. Do you see it?

> "'The Lord himself goes before you and will be with you; he will never leave you nor forsake you. Do not be afraid; do not be discouraged.'"
> (Deuteronomy 31:8 NIV)

He can be trusted.

But He can't be surprised.

I find immense comfort in this. I hope you do too.

* What has surprised you lately?
* What has God provided for you that reminded you of His sovereignty?
* How can you be more trusting of God?

What Do Your Books Say About You?

What do your books say about you?

They say, "Don't judge a book by its cover."

But can you judge someone by what books they read? (More on that in a minute.)

We found the house we want. I love everything about it. I just got a feeling, you know?

I didn't even open a drawer and I knew it was for me. It just felt right. I could see my family there.

I know some people don't move forward with a purchase until they check every little nook and cranny, consider everything that could possibly go wrong. And then think, think, and think some more before making a decision. That is one way of doing it. Also, that may be considered the *better* way by some.

Well, that is not me.

I walked in and said, "Let's make an offer."

I guess I was judging the house by its entryway. Is that the same as judging a book by its cover?

I don't know. It's just how I do things. Call it intuition, call it the Holy Spirit—it has worked for me.

I called my husband, and he asked about the kitchen (he's the cook). I said, "What? I don't know, I didn't even look really." My goal was to make sure there was a swimming pool.

Since my husband wasn't there when I decided we were buying it, we had to go back and see it together. We lingered. Sat on couches. Stood at the sink in the kitchen. I even opened a drawer. We walked around the yard, the pool, and garage. Everything just solidified my initial reaction. This feels like home.

We went into the office which is lined with bookshelves. They were full, which I love because books make me feel safe and comfortable and I need to have space for them. I walked up close to see what books were on the shelves. I got goosebumps.

Does this really tell us anything?

I think it does.

First, THE BIBLE. Not one. Two. To me, this says we love Jesus. You know how people have scrapbooks telling the story of their lives? To me, the people that have the Bible out in their home are saying, "This is our story. This is who we are."

Second, the Air Force Academy books. Military. Patriots. To me, this says they are trustworthy, disciplined, honorable, people of their word. Interestingly, we bought our first house in our previous community from a military man, a Naval aviator. That was the right decision too.

And the dictionary. Words. Old school. Traditional. I have to admit I'm a little skeptical of people who read everything on the Kindle or the iPad. I mean, don't you want to hold the book? Don't you want to feel it and smell it? (It's true. I smell books. My friends

I used to work with would look at me like I was nuts, but I need the whole sensory experience.)

Having said all of that, I'm also in the habit of googling definitions and spellings so I contradict myself. But the dictionary made me think of my dad, a different age, a slower pace.

All of this made me think of my dad. A Marine, a lifelong Catholic, a man of words, and a man of his word.

It was like he was there, encouraging me, nodding yes.

I'm telling y'all. I found my home.

* When have you judged a book by its cover?
* What could someone learn about you if they saw your bookshelf?
* What kind of a decision maker are you?

Middle School and Life

I had my first school parent coffee in Texas.

Yep, that's right. I did it. I checked in, showed my license, put on my name tag, and entered the scariest place of all—the middle school lunchroom.

I have to say it has gotten much better. It's still not easy, but I'm okay. I can enter without the panic of *Who will I sit with?*

Being new to town and the school and the state and well...just *new* in that way that feels sort of confusing but also funny because there is no way you can hide it. I mean, I walked in, started wandering around, and a teacher asked me, "Are you lost?"

And I thought about answering, *Honey, you don't know the half of it.* Literally, just getting to the school was a major feat. Needing to know where the lunchroom is way beyond. I just can't.

So, it's obvious.

Thank God I ran into someone I did know right away. By saying I know her, I mean I met her once and I thought it was her so I approached and thank God she recognized me and we started chatting. I guess maybe the lunchroom hasn't changed that much. We still look for someone to sit with. I've just become much braver. And wiser. And more comfortable in my skin. Which takes a lot of years of walking into the lunchroom, board room, dorm room, new job, new neighborhood...you get my point.

The principal started talking, and I realized that this school, this experience, this whole Texas thing...is different. He said he started in education in 1953. I was doing the math in my head when he clarified, that's when he started *first grade*. And he said he has loved education ever since. His title is Dr. so I know he's gone to a lot of schooling, but I couldn't give a hoot. (Don't I sound southern already?) I was more interested in what he said about the *culture* and how important it is to him. He talked about when he was a principal before, and he was widowed and he suffered so much. He just couldn't do it anymore, so he retired. He said he couldn't "run the race" anymore.

He said he was blessed to find a wonderful woman who is his wife now, and she brought him back. She reminded him of how much he loved being in education, so he came out of retirement. He said school is important and he loves it, but he loves his wife and family more. That school and learning and accomplishing and all that we do here in this building is really, really important but not as important as your family.

He assured us that even though the school is new, and the technology doesn't work yet and there is confusion and the buses are late...the teachers love our kids and are trying their best and working really hard. He asked for our patience and asked if we could please encourage and support the teachers. He reminded us that we are all in this together.

A mom shared that her daughter was not allowed to go to the bathroom because she didn't have a "pass" so she had an accident. He was mortified and so sorry. He launched into this whole thing.

He said there are two camps: "Rules and Regs" and "Culture." He said he's not much of a "rules and reg" guy, but he knows they are necessary. He's more into relationships and getting people what they need and *offering grace.*

Of course, this made me cry. *Me too!* I wanted to shout! *Me too! Amen!*

There were moms there of course who kept pressing about bathroom passes and the buses and complaining about homework. I was having an out-of-body experience. I was watching and listening and I wanted to shout! *Did you hear him?! We are offering GRACE. It's about GRACE! All are doing their best!*

Now don't get me wrong—parents have every right to ask all those questions. All the administrators there were lovely and accommodating and tried their best to help everyone.

It just reminded me of how we sometimes get about religion and God. We put all the rules and regulations in. We start keeping score. We demand. We perform. We measure. We get so tired we can't "run the race" anymore. We forget that we are in this together. We get so worried about people having a "pass" that we don't see they are about to have an accident right in front of us. We don't recognize the suffering. We make them jump through hoops. We abandon. We criticize. We humiliate. This is love? This is Christian living?

But then Jesus comes in with, "Hey, guess what? I'm not much of a rules and reg guy. I'm here to offer grace." He assures us that He loves us and He's for us and He cares about our *culture.* He sets us *free.* To go to the bathroom or whatever. He says, "You don't need a pass...I AM THE PASS!" You are all good.

So at the end of an hour of people questioning and complaining, a woman stood up. She said, "I want to thank you. For coming in here and talking about *culture* and *grace* and for making it a priority to make this a *good and kind* place that offers understanding and support and encouragement."

Actually, I have no idea what else she said. But she was tracking with what I was feeling and a lot of other people in the room. I couldn't even hear her.

I was crying Holy Spirit tears and shaking my head and saying, "Amen!"

Because honestly, he's a principal but he's also a missionary. Right here. In Texas. In the middle school lunchroom.

It *was* a lunchroom.

But honestly, it felt more like church.

* Are you a "Rules and Regs" person, a "Culture" person, or a combination?
* When is it okay to break the rules?
* Where have you experienced good leadership in your community?

The Finish Line

I want to share everything with you but obviously that is not possible, and you would not want to know it all. Like the fact that the air conditioning is out in our corporate rental apartment. Did I mention it's HOT in Texas?

But I see God's hand everywhere. I mean, the other day I was trying to explain to a dad I met that we feel welcome here, that everyone is friendly and helpful.

He said, "Yeah, you know, we are all just trying to help each other over the finish line."

How much do you love that little tidbit!?

Praise God! Because I feel like I'm nowhere near the finish line. I feel like the one who is running around looking around *trying to figure out what lane she is in* and if she has the right shoes on.

This is beginner Texas, y'all. I mean Texas 101.

In a meeting at school today the people all looked so kind, and they were helpful and friendly, but they had to explain a lot to me. They said, "Well, in Texas...things are a little different," many times. There are new terms and new rules. I'm learning my way around schools and town and I still can't find the Nordstrom that they swear is here. (Side note. I found Nordstrom. But before that, I found J. Crew and started tearing up. My daughter took a picture of me pointing to the sign and smiling like a lunatic.)

But even in my lost-ness, I feel found. Even while I have no permanent residence, I feel at home.

I tried to explain this to my friend, that people are different here. And she said maybe that's true, but *maybe you are different there.*

God shows you who you are when you have to go. He shows you what you need when you only get a suitcase and a carry-on. He shows you what's important when there is too much to do so you can't do it all and you must choose. He shows you who *He* is when you admit you need Him.

How I've hidden behind my things. My comfort. My pride. My accomplishments. My *knowing.* How comfortable I have been in my safe, beautiful home knowing my neighbors and feeling so connected. I worked hard to build up that kind of comfort, that rootedness, that stability. I have put my trust in things and people and the world. Oh, how complacent I had become.

I enter this new adventure with eyes wide open. To who I am, who I have been, who I want to be. And *whose* I am.

I am God's. His daughter. His beloved. Chosen. Protected. Enough. I am His. He will provide for me.

He gives moments of encouragement from others. I was in the parking lot of the high school belly laughing with another mom this morning whom I had not ever laid eyes on before today. I call that a candy kiss from God.

I met one woman early on and I love her! I keep running into her. Last night at a school meeting where God must have known I'd like a friendly face to sit with, there she was.

He says, "Follow Me and I will lead you." When I think of that now, I don't picture the disciples leaving their fishing nets. I picture my family. On the plane to Texas. With our suitcases and backpacks. And our prayers. Our trust. Our belief.

It's true sometimes when you are most lost is the time when God is closest to you.

When you are untethered to worldly possessions, you hold on tightly to Him. He is steady.

Protecting. Providing. Placing kind people in your path.

Preparing you for the day when He will carry you over that finish line.

- ✳ What have you placed your trust in other than God?
- ✳ How has God shown you that you can trust Him?
- ✳ When have you had to let go of people, places, or things?

STICKING WITH GRACE

Lord, keep reminding us. Keep bringing us back. Keep us on track. Help us always to return to You. Help us stick with grace.

We read a lot and listen to podcasts and talk to friends and watch TV and stream shows and spend time on social media. And it's so noisy out there. There are so many choices. Help us stick with grace.

Continue to teach us, Lord. Convict us. Help us discern what is right and good in Your eyes. Give us courage to choose You every time. Help us stick with grace.

In a world that is loud and demanding and punishing, help us hear Your voice above all others. Lead us to an abundant life. Help us stick with grace.

We love You, we praise You, we trust You. Amen.

Time for a Reset

I'm feeling nostalgic. Did you ever lie on a blanket under the stars and just look up, no agenda, no phone, no rush? Remember when reading a book didn't seem like a monumental task? I love books! But now it's difficult to concentrate for more than a few minutes at a time. Remember when people were kind and intelligent and took time to think before they spoke? I miss those days.

I also remember our family around a table talking and laughing. I remember road trips (long road trips!) with just the radio and books. "I'm bored," I would say. And my mom would say, "Only boring people are bored." So I would look out the window and imagine.

I remember long drawn-out card games and puzzles, and my older brothers teaching me to play pool and ping pong. I remember sunsets when no one had a phone with them, and sunrises that felt like a personal one-on-one with God, no need to record or post, that would only cheapen it.

I remember phone calls with the spiral cord pulled tight so I could go in my room for privacy. I would talk to friends for hours on the phone, no rush. All before call-waiting became a thing and if someone called our house it would ring "busy." I remember thinking call waiting was so rude. Does anyone even know what is rude anymore? Now people wear watches that alert them every second about a news story or a text. They are out to lunch or dinner with friends, but they are constantly looking at their watch. It's astonishing. What could be that urgent?

Do you remember having to call a friend and say hello to her parents on the phone? Or did you have to answer your own home phone saying, "Hello, Koach residence, this is Sue speaking." I remember calling my parents from my summer abroad. It was very rare and expensive to call, and it was a big deal with an operator speaking Spanish. Now we just text from all over the world. Most people don't even have home phones anymore.

I remember waiting for my pictures to be developed at Walgreens, getting so excited to pick them up, and then realizing there was only one good one in the whole bunch.

As I'm writing this, I see the theme. We used to wait. We had to be patient, polite, and present.

Was it always better? No. Progress is good. But I worry that we are rushing through life distracted. I'm afraid we will miss it. Or just collapse from the mental and emotional exhaustion.

This isn't about limiting phone and screen time. Although that would certainly be a good thing.

This is about not settling. This is about owning the fact that we deserve more than this treadmill we are on. Something's gotta give. It's time for a reset.

Stop settling for a life of fast food, short tweets, rushed days, distracted relationships, temporary thrills, and knee-jerk reactions. You were made for more.

You are a masterpiece created in God's image. We all are. And yet, here we are scrolling social media for hours a day, letting the nonsense invade our hearts, minds, and souls.

Why have we settled for a life of distraction and irritation and hurry over the beauty of stillness, peace, and presence? Do you feel this?

Where did we get off track?

Were we off track before the lockdowns, fear, and upheaval of the Covid restrictions? Even if we were, there is no doubt that it has gotten worse. There is a collective anxiety, and it's reaching fever pitch. We can only take so much. We were not meant to carry the weight of the world on our shoulders! I've talked to so many people who say they are distracted and irritable and unmotivated. We can't settle for this.

This is not who we are! We have to remember that we are children of God, and we are here with a purpose. We can't waste any more time.

It's okay. We can grab ahold of the time we have left. We can insist on being mindful and intentional. We can break out of the prison we've created for ourselves.

Step one: find some time today to sit quietly by yourself and do nothing. It will feel strange. Don't have your phone near you. Turn off all external stimulation. Remember how it feels to breathe. Let your mind wander. Remember who you are when it's just you. This is the beginning of the reset.

※ What thoughts have you been avoiding through distraction?

※ What comes up for you when you sit quietly by yourself?

※ How will you eliminate hurry and chaos from your life?

Let's Not Glamorize Misery

I've been reading and watching and listening to what's out there on social media and podcasts and books and TV shows and something is rising up in me. It's a protective spirit, an "Oh no way! Not on my watch" energy. Here's how I'm feeling...

What is this nonsense?

We are so afraid of being positive.

We are so afraid of saying we are not afraid. Why?

Why does someone on Instagram say, "I know we are still breathing, but we are all dead inside, right?" get over 124,000 likes but someone sharing hope gets ignored or maybe just a shoulder shrug and some judgment?

I just heard a woman say on a podcast, "I am dead a lot inside." She talked so much about not knowing who she was. (bingo – identity is everything!) And "I wouldn't mind getting hit by a bus. This is too much. Send a wolf over here. End this." She continues, "I don't know why I'm here anymore; I don't know what the point of my f—--- life is." Her cohost just murmured, "Mmmm."

WHAT?

Is this profound? Is this helpful? Is she trying to be funny? This has to be a joke, right?

No, she is serious.

People are building platforms and businesses around misery and depression and lack of purpose. It is astounding. And tragic.

When I listen to and read about all the women in their 20s, 30s, 40s, saying how sad they are, how much they struggle looking in the mirror, how much they don't want to get out of bed, I feel like we are in a *state of emergency.*

The people to get us out of it are not the government, the doctors, big pharma, big tech. The people who we need to show up and be loud are the older women. Women who have experienced life.

Us. You and me. We have to lead. We are here for such a time as this.

Let's talk about the ebbs and flows.

Let's talk about "this too shall pass."

Let's talk about Jesus.

Let's talk about Identity.

Let's talk about speaking our minds.

Let's talk about setting boundaries.

Let's talk about hope.

Let's talk about joy.

Let's talk about service.

Let's talk about laughter.

Let's talk about loving people.

Let's talk about having fun.

Let's talk about original design.

Let's normalize strength and resilience and tenacity.

Let's talk about the difference between having a feeling and letting that feeling define us.

Let's not glamorize misery. I know it's all the rage to show up vulnerable and broken. But I'm calling it. That's enough.

As my mom would say, "Honey, that's unbecoming." And then she would remind me, "Wash your face, put some lipstick on, go get a Diet Coke, and get out in the world." Because some things aren't that deep. They aren't meant to be dwelled upon. Sure, we go there. We are human. We live in the real world and some days stink. But we don't stay there. And we don't let people we love stay there either.

Find something you love.

Find something to do.

Find someone to serve.

A life that's all about you and your feelings is sure to leave you empty.

Women, let's step up when we hear this language. Let's answer back to this cry for help. Let's not just nod our heads in agreement and solemnly go along with lies that are holding young women captive. I know you want to be compassionate. I know you want to validate their feelings. I know you want to make sure they feel seen and heard. You can do all that and speak truth into their hearts and minds. Don't hold back what you know because the voices of misery in this culture are loud and defensive, daring you to defy them.

Do it. Defy them.

A whisper of hope is a million times more powerful than a shout of despair.

* What hope can you offer young people today?
* In what ways can you be a leader right now, right where you are?
* What lies from the culture are you believing?

Feeling Left Out

Oh, the lies and bill of goods we have been sold. Popularity, being liked, getting likes. We place so much importance on things that don't matter in the long run.

Facebook plays into all our insecurities and *fomo* (fear of missing out). We see the beautiful pictures of our friends laughing and spending time together without us. Or we hear a story about something fun that happened, and we wonder why we weren't invited. We worry that we won't pass muster. Or that our husband doesn't. Or our kids. We let bitterness take root. We lose confidence, and we withdraw. But we still see and hear which just feels like a dumping on our heads of heavy rejection.

Heck, sometimes there's nothing even going on, and we only perceive the slight. Maybe we've been rejected in the past, so we assume we are being rejected now. Maybe we don't believe we are worthy of being invited.

This is not our inheritance. Jesus did not die on a cross for us so we would sit home feeling lonely and isolated. He invites us into belonging.

You may feel like the beautiful people are out without you. Maybe they are, but who cares? I have been with that crew. It's exhausting. All that time spent planning and maneuvering and manipulating and posturing. And for what? Shiny parties end. Often all you're left with is a hangover. Just because you get invited doesn't mean you won't carry around a gut-wrenching feeling of loneliness anyway.

My wise mom once told me, "In your 20s and 30s you want to be invited everywhere. Once you hit 40, you just hope and pray the phone doesn't ring." So true! Yet even when we are older and wiser, not being invited can still sting.

Maybe you have felt rejected at church. It seems wrong, but I've talked to enough people and been around enough churches to know that no place is immune to cliques and judgments and people performing and jockeying for a spot at the top. Maybe your feeling of rejection comes from your career or your ministry. Maybe you feel like you have been passed over. Maybe you see other people succeeding, and you wonder why it's not you. Maybe you have heard criticism of your work, or your ideas have been mocked. Maybe you feel like nobody believes in your dreams. Maybe you feel invisible.

Here's the BIG T Truth. God sees you. God loves you. God chooses you. He calls you worthy.

Train your thoughts to return to that Truth.

He not only understands your dreams and the desires of your heart, but He also put them there!

Remind yourself. He is your audience. He is cheering from the front row. He believes in you.

He *is* the cool group. He will lead you to the place you want to be. He says you are amazing. He wants your heart and your time. He invites you into a relationship with Him.

No other invitation can compare. No party shines like His. No feast is bigger. No man loves like Him. No dance partner is as captivating. No calling is greater than the one He gives to you. No other celebration *lasts forever.*

Friends, *you are invited*. Will you sit around with *fomo* about earthly things that are temporary and unfulfilling, or will you say a Great Big Yes to the invitation that will transform your life?

* What is God inviting you into right now?

* When have you felt rejected, and how did you handle that?

* What matters most to you in the long run?

Belly Laughs

We need sun. We chased it all the way to this beautiful, faraway, no cars allowed, feels like Survivor Island. And we found it. For two days. And then on the third day, the rains came.

I prayed to God for sun on that third day. My mom was arriving on the island, and we were preparing by shouting out, "The plane, the plane!"

I prayed my mom would arrive to find sunny skies. The winter had been so long for all of us. It's the third day! We needed rebirth, restoration, and resurrection.

God had other plans. He agreed with the part about rebirth, but He didn't see the sun as an integral part of that.

He chose rain.

It poured. Puddles were everywhere. There was a reprieve when we met my mom at the dock, and she got off the ferry. We ate cheeseburgers inside the restaurant. It was good to be together. It was evening and pitch-black outside. No light pollution on the island. Probably because there are no lights!

We didn't all fit in the golf cart on the way home, so my husband walked in the pouring rain while I drove my kids and my mom. We zipped through puddles using a flashlight to just barely light the way. We were getting splashed. My mom thought something was biting her. We had her luggage. She kept saying, "Are we almost there?" It was hilarious. The laughing and screaming and everyone telling me where to go and me getting lost was perfect. My stomach hurt from laughing so much. I haven't laughed that hard in years.

There is no way I could have planned that moment. Sometimes I don't know what I need, so I pray for things like sunshine. But He knows and He brings the bigger things like laughter and moments that I know for sure none of us will ever forget.

And today He woke me up with a bright, sunny morning. There it is. The sun. And a dull ache in my abs from laughing.

Grace abounds.

* What are you trying to control instead of just being present in the moment?
* What has God shown you when you have surrendered to His plans?
* Write about a memory you have that showed you a new way of thinking and being.

The Mirror Moment

I don't know anymore.

I hear them say the country is going to hell in a handbasket. And I think, but God...

I listen to reports of protesting and fear and anger. People imagining a particular outcome is certain doom. And I think, but God...

I hear of church corruption and abuse and people hurt by those they trusted for guidance. And I think, but God...

I learn about sex trafficking and horrible dark crimes happening on the sunny streets near me. And I think, but God...

We can wrap ourselves in anxiety and agree to be victims. We can get worked up and forget that we belong to each other. We can dehumanize others so we can easily hate and call it just. But God...

God says we are victorious. He says we are beloved. He assures us we are enough. He implores us not to be afraid. He tells us to be bold and courageous and kind.

Jesus teaches us to love our neighbors as ourselves.

So first, love yourself. Call yourself worthy. Look in the mirror. Take a good long look and get right with that person. Hurt people hurt people. And hurt people herd people. I remember when I first heard this. I thought of all the times when I was hurt and tried to gather people to my side. I "herded" people to be on my team and make me feel justified in my hurt and sometimes maybe even come along with me seeking revenge or lashing out. Ugh. Don't do that.

My friend says, "Go to the throne, not the phone." A good reminder.

Heal your hurt. Invite the Lord in to minister to your heart. Get free.

Listen to the soft whisper of grace and dance in the cool breeze of freedom. Then don't forget it. Return to the well for Living Water. Every day. Every minute. You will need it. Drench yourself in the Spirit of God. Stay free.

Remember that every single soul on earth needs that same mirror moment. Just like you. They are not the devil. They are human. They need God. They long for Hope. They hunger for Peace. Offer peace. And kindness and grace. Offer to others what you have been so freely given.

We can't see God's actual hand of protection and love and provision in some of our current political discussions, but we can see and hear *you*. How are you representing that soft whisper of grace and that cool breeze of freedom?

Don't just talk about what you want. Be what you want. Show others what's possible. No fear. Just love. We need you. Go ahead...Lead.

* How can you represent God well in the public discourse of today?
* Write about a "But God" moment in your life.
* What does it look like to stay hopeful in today's world?

Waiting Is a Verb

A wise friend told me the truth yesterday.

She said I might have to just wait.

Then she told me that waiting is a verb.

I asked God to show me what He means by waiting. Actually, I asked Google to show me what God says about waiting. Google and God gave me this.

> "We pray that you'll have the strength to stick it out over the long haul—not the grim strength of gritting your teeth but the glory-strength God gives. It is strength that endures the unendurable and spills over into joy,
>
> thanking the Father who makes us strong enough to take part in everything bright and beautiful that he has for us.
>
> God rescued us from dead-end alleys and dark dungeons. He's set us up in the kingdom of the Son he loves so much." (Colossians 1:11 MSG)

I cried.

Yes! Yes! That's what I want. I want to stop gritting my teeth and experience the glory-strength of God.

I want my life, all of it, even the waiting, to spill over into joy. I want to experience everything bright and beautiful that God has for me.

Lord, help us to go easy in the waiting. Remind us that waiting is doing something if we surrender it to You. Remind me that surrender is not giving up.

In our waiting, God is working.

Another friend told me once, "When you surrender, you join the winning team."

Yes, Lord. Victory is mine. Maybe not right this minute, but it's coming.

Thank you.

* What does surrender mean to you?
* When has God asked you to wait?
* What Scripture gives you encouragement when you are waiting?

Quiet

I'm practicing being quiet.

The other day I received an email that a teacher from my children's school had been killed in a car accident. Right up the road from where I live. On a corner I maneuver every day. I read it on my phone as I was wandering around my house doing dishes and laundry, breathing easy, drinking coffee. I sat down and wept.

We just never know.

And people at their Christmas party in California. A mad man and his wife come in, terrorists with guns intent on killing. More weeping.

School shootings.

Mothers I know, mourning. Mothers I don't know. Terrified.

And all the people. Talking, tweeting, scrolling Facebook and Instagram. It's so LOUD.

I told my husband that day that I felt like I was on a speeding train, and I couldn't stop it.

The TV. For goodness sake, the twenty-four-hour news cycle. Mayhem and misery. Opinions and anger. Wild speculation and irresponsible reporting.

I long for the good ol' days of three channels and static after a certain hour. A time when the world would sleep.

Just stop.

Tired and weary, I took a nap.

> "You'll take afternoon naps without a worry, you'll enjoy a good night's sleep. No need to panic over alarms or surprises, or predictions that doomsday's just around the corner, Because God will be right there with you; he'll keep you safe and sound."
>
> (Proverbs 3:24-26 MSG)

I told my daughter this. I explained that I heard bad news and there was so much it made me cry. I didn't know what to do so I napped. She smiled and kind of chuckled, almost like, "Wow, you can do that? Is that an option?"

Oh, yes, it's an option. We don't always have to form an opinion or an argument. We don't always have to come out swinging or go down broken. We don't always have to get louder. Just because we don't weigh in on every topic doesn't mean we don't care. It means we care a lot. And we are *listening*.

We get to choose our response.

Sometimes the most loving thing we can do is weep. And nap.

I surely think God understands. He weeps too. And as we nap, He stays awake and watchful. He sees everything.

Trusting Him today. And tomorrow. And forever.

Amen.

* What does rest mean to you?
* How do you practice self-care?
* Write a prayer for the world.

When Did I Stop Playing?

I made a huge discovery when I was in training to teach yoga for kids.

We talked about play and how important it is. One of our assignments was to play for twenty minutes.

Oh my gosh, this was eye-opening!

I decided to swim. It was October but I live in Texas, and we have a pool and it's 94 degrees, so, why not?

Picture this: it's midday and I decide to put on my swimsuit and frolic in the pool for no reason but to play. To say this felt weird is an understatement. I was thinking, *What if someone stops by?* I felt like I was wasting time. I had no purpose. My mind was telling me, *Just swim some laps so you can count this as exercise.*

You guys. When did this happen?

When did I start needing to account for every minute of the day? Why was I in the pool feeling like I should be doing laundry or at least reading a book or something? Weren't there colleges to research and wasn't there grocery shopping to be done? *How were my kids going to turn out if they found their mom went swimming alone midday?*

Honestly. When did I become the party-pooper?

So, I forced myself and started shooting some hoops. I am so bad. I can't make a basket to save my life despite having played center in junior high. And my dad called me Kareem which is hilarious because my main role on the team was to lead the cheers. I actually fouled out most games.

I swam a little and immediately became winded, so I started doing handstands and talking to myself underwater... "Scooby Doo." Did you do that? Say things underwater to your friends and make them guess what you said? We had categories. I was playing TV shows. By myself.

I did some flips, but my ears filled up with water, so I stopped.

At one point I chuckled to myself thinking about how long it had been since I just played for no reason. How long it had been since I had gone in the pool with no regard for how my thighs looked or if my hair was going to get gross or if getting wet was worth it because then I have to shower and get dressed again.

When did this happen?

Years ago.

I sidelined myself years ago.

If I was doing something active, it was for a workout. I would walk or run or go to the gym. I went because it was good for me, and I wanted to stay healthy. I wouldn't say any of that was fun. Even my yoga, which I love so much, has become a "have-to" in my mind. I was thinking of it from a teaching perspective, and I forgot how much I enjoy it.

How does this happen?

I had seen my husband go up on the side of the hot tub and slide down into the pool. There is no slide; he just made up something fun. Imagine that? (Side note: He has not sidelined himself. Ever. He puts on his swimsuit every day after work and jumps in. He likes the back runs of the ski mountain. He's gone skydiving. Friends that went to Mexico with us can attest to the fact that he likes to jump off cliffs, and now in Texas, he's taking up hunting and fishing. If there's a game or activity happening, he is in. (Is this a gender thing?) Anyway, I went in the hot tub and then slid into the pool. It was fun and refreshing, and I startled myself thinking, *I want to do that again!*

When my husband came home and saw a beach towel out and the basketball in the pool, he asked the kids, "Did you swim today?"

They said, "No, Mom did."

He was incredulous. And envious. He kept saying, "I always want you to swim with me. Why don't you swim with me?"

Ugh. Why don't I? What the heck have I been doing? Was I too busy to have fun? Is he thinking, *Where is the fun girl I married?!*

I tried to hold my breath and swim across the pool underwater without coming up for air. It reminded me of the many long summer days spent in the pool. Hours and hours of mindless fun, pruney skin and green hair. We would leave the pool sun-drenched and exhausted. The next day we would ride our bikes in a pack to do it again. The pool always signified freedom. Summer. Friends. Long, lazy days of nothing.

I'm convinced God can do amazing things in those lazy days. He is the Author of freedom.

We spend all this time reading and writing and working and studying and striving and not wasting a precious minute. And yet, He beckons, put that down, come outside, swim with Me. I want to see you laugh and play and be free.

Yesterday, I said yes, and I could feel His delight.

* What do you do for fun?
* When was the last time you played for no reason other than to play?
* In what ways have you sidelined yourself?

Limitations as Invitations

In my yoga teacher training, we learned this: "Limitations in our lives equate to freedom."

We were talking about physical limitations relating to yoga, but honestly, that statement just blew me away. The truth is that when we accept our limits and need to lean into God's strength and power, we are transformed.

We all have limitations in our lives. If we listened to the world, we would see these limitations as roadblocks. We could (and some of us have) allowed these limitations to defeat us. We throw up our hands and say, "Well, I can't do that thing (fill in the blank) because I'm too weak, poor, sick, heavy, uneducated, unfit, scared, busy, (fill in the blank)."

Since we all endure different limitations (they can be physical, emotional, spiritual) and we all have unique dreams, let me just get general with this statement, "I can't fulfill my life's dream because I am *too weak in some way; I'm lacking something.*"

So we give up.

This is where we may go if we see *limitations* as roadblocks.

But here's the thing.

We are all lacking something.

Even the people that have fulfilled their dreams. Even the people you think have it all together. Even the people you see chasing their dreams right now.

Saying you don't have it all together is not admitting defeat. It is declaring *victory*! It brings *freedom*.

Freedom from pretending and wearing a false mask and playing God and striving for control. It means freedom from our sins and our weaknesses and our addictions. It means that we aren't *supposed to* be able to do everything perfectly. When we admit we have limitations and we need God, we can rest and be free from needing to please and protect and be all things to all people. We accept God's grace. We offer ourselves grace. We go out into the world and offer grace to others.

> "Because of the extravagance of those revelations, and so I wouldn't get a big head, I was given the gift of a handicap to keep me in constant touch with my limitations. Satan's angel did his best to get me down; what he in fact did was push me to my knees. No danger then of walking around high and mighty! At first I didn't think of it as a gift, and begged God to remove it. Three times I did that, and then he told me,
>
> My grace is enough; it's all you need.
>
> My strength comes into its own in your weakness.
>
> Once I heard that, I was glad to let it happen. I quit focusing on the handicap and began appreciating the gift. It was a case of Christ's strength moving in on my weakness. Now I take limitations in stride, and with good cheer, these limitations that cut me down

to size—abuse, accidents, opposition, bad breaks. I just let Christ take over! And so the weaker I get, the stronger I become." (2 Corinthians 12:7-10 MSG)

To stand before the Lord and say,

Yeah, guess what, Lord? I don't have it all together. I am not perfect. I can't figure it out, fix it, mend it, create it, or heal it on my own. I need You. I can't make good choices all the time. Honestly, Lord, I'm not sure which one is the good choice sometimes.

I can't keep my kids from harm. I can't save people. I can't save myself. My humanness keeps getting in the way.

I don't want to say I can't do it all because this world has taught me that admitting weakness means I am, well, weak. A fate worse than death here in America, Lord. We are bred to brag and achieve and compete and strive and gain and accomplish and never, ever let anyone see us sweat.

Lord, I ask You to remove that burden from us. It's just so tiring, Lord. Take it away. Teach us the Truth. You came to turn this world upside down. You came and did a new thing. You said the weak will become strong. You said blessed are the poor in Spirit. You, Lord, came and washed feet. You were a servant. You did not demand a King's robe and crown of jewels. You came as a vulnerable baby and died under a crown of thorns.

Lord, it is really hard for us to let go of what we have learned from this world. We don't like our limitations. We don't like it when we feel weak. We are uncomfortable asking for help. We think we long for perfection. We think we long to be rulers of our own little kingdoms, but, Lord, You know what we really want is peace and joy and love everlasting. We want the freedom that comes from You.

So we have limitations. We are human. You are God and we are not. Gosh, what a relief. Can we rest now? Can we just open our hands and accept Your grace? You've got this, right? You've got my life and my kids and my marriage and my friendships and my health and my life's work and my needs. You have this, right? It's okay if I'm not perfect?

Lord, help me today to accept my limitations as an invitation to draw near to You. Help me to say yes to You so I can taste the freedom that comes from laying this heavy burden of perfection down. Set me free. Please, Lord, set me free.

Amen.

* What are some of your limitations?
* In what ways do you need to rely on God's strength?
* When have you experienced difficulty in admitting your limitations?

GRACE IN COMMUNITY

Lord, thank you for our communities. Thank you for the people You have put in my life.

I think about the women who have sat in circles with me and studied God's Word. The women who have shared with vulnerability and who have prayed with fervor. I think about the people who have laughed with me my whole life, people who have spent time with me just having fun and hanging out. What a gift that is. I think about the friends who taught me about God by their easy way, the kindness in their smile, the generosity in their spirit.

I can picture my friends who taught, served, and gave of themselves from a yoga mat, stage, non-profit fundraiser, school board meeting, Bible study taught from a living room couch. How each in their own way brought a little slice of God's grace to me. How they ministered to my heart. Their presence built me up. I thank you, Lord, for knowing what I need and giving it to me so often through Your people.

Oh, Lord, help us build and create spaces that feel like a warm hug for others. Help us be calm for each other as the storm rages outside. Help us be light in darkness, strength in a weary world, comfort in a time of need. And pure joy-filled, light-bearing, celebrators when the occasion calls for it.

As we look back at our story, give us a spirit of compassion and forgiveness and understanding for the times when communities, churches, or people have failed us. Or when we have been on the outside feeling forgotten. Forgive us for the times we have been less than kind. Give us courage to be the designers of a new kind of community based on Your love.

Thank you for what You are building. We are honored to be a part of it. Amen.

Church

I believe in one God, Father Almighty, Creator of Heaven and Earth, of all that is seen and unseen.

We profess our faith.

I wondered if the prayers mattered. If we even knew what we were saying, just reciting out of memory.

I listened to the drone of the crowd, the monotone voices not raised in song but rather mumbling or is that humming?

Agnus Dei...I listened in awe as my kids chanted along, having been taught the words I did not know. They skipped that for a few years in catechism, right when I would have learned it, I guess.

The incense and the holy water. We sign the cross.

The God who made me, the God who saved me, the God who lives within me.

The movements are fluid, practiced, habitual. The feeling gone, the arm, the heart, the head not syncing.

What time is it?

Did I bring any money for the collection?

Our Father, who art in heaven, hallowed be Thy name. Thy kingdom come, Thy will be done...

Taking comfort in the words Jesus taught. Looking for links to Jesus—beautiful, radical Son of God— to this, now, with my family fussing in a pew, bored.

Listening intently for wisdom, insight, life. Craving freedom, redemption...a Word from God that I was okay, that we are all okay, that it was going to be okay.

Glory be to the Father and the Son and the Holy Spirit...

I'm hungry and tired...that girl's outfit is cute...what am I thinking? Focus.

Forgive me Father for I have sinned in my thoughts, in my words, in what I have done and what I have failed to do...

I have failed.

I long to worship...to throw my hands up in exuberant dance and sing with freedom about the grace that saved me. I long for grace to save me.

Peace be with you. And with your Spirit, they say...What? Since when? Why? And also with you, I say clumsily and look away.

I think about other churches where they cross the aisle, the peace takes a long time, and no one cares. They hug and laugh and smile and meet. Maybe that's the grace that saves them. Maybe I want what they have. I start to criticize our way. I want more. I look at my watch. Are we almost done?

We look away politely and hurry to our knees.

Do this in remembrance of me...there He is...His words and His sacrifice...so unbelievable. So profound. So necessary.

My knees seem the only place for me to be at a time like this. Heads are bowed in thanksgiving, reverence, awe...You did this for me? For me? Oh, grace that saved me.

Said time and time again across the world...His words...the ones He said to His disciples...I look around...do people really get this? Do I? If we did, we would be clamoring to get at the body and blood of our Savior. We have learned restraint, we have put up walls, we wait until we are told to exit the pew. It is all very dignified. So well-behaved. I'm so used to it. Those life-changing words have become ordinary, regular, known.

I make an effort to listen, to really hear...what was Jesus saying? Why? What does it mean?

Go in peace to love and serve the world.

We enter a barn-style building with lights and a sound system... the worship band is on fire...we sing loud, and we raise our hands and we move and laugh and drink coffee. I cry with the words because I love Jesus.

The preacher is a teacher who is passionate and brilliant and funny and gifted. He knows the Bible and Jesus and he preaches to our hearts, and we swell with emotion. He wears jeans and tells jokes, and we can relate. He is married and has children.

We bring our Bibles and read along and mark in the margins and we learn and grow.

The Spirit is so tangible, I get goosebumps and feel full. I am ready to go in peace to love and serve the world.

My friend asks me if I feel guilty for "leaving." I am not surprised by the question, but I am a little by my answer. No. But do you call it leaving? I mean, really, can you leave?

The imagery, the art, the stories, the icons…the imagination of the church will always be a part of me. The ceremony and sacraments and the smells and sights of your life…do you leave that? Would anyone ever just pack their bags and turn around and light a match? I would not. I will not.

For so long I thought I needed to decide…that there was a right way to worship, and I would find it. That there would be a moment of clarity and I would make some grand statement about finding the perfect church. I spent years defending the faith of my childhood and years criticizing it. I have done both in the same breath.

But what I know now is that people are messy, and religion is a people business. There will never be a perfect way to worship. It's like learning in school. Many of us learn differently, but all of us learn. We must find our own way. So we ask for help and guidance. But people have opinions and agendas. I have opinions and agendas.

So we ask God. Show me. We read God's Word and we pray and spend time alone with Jesus and we ask Him…Where do You want me? How can I grow? Where can it be more about You?

And then we listen. And we go. And we realize it won't be perfect…but God, He is after us. He will use all means to reach us. He will lead us.

The more we talk to Him, the more we can find Him everywhere.

There is not only one way. It's not one or the other.

It's *both*, it's *and*, it's *all*.

My kids ask questions. They want to know if everyone knows the "Our Father." I say yes because it's the prayer Jesus taught us, and we all believe in Jesus. We are more alike than different. They press. What about communion? Is it a symbol? What about the Bible? Which one do we read?

I love the questions, the interest. They are awake. Their faith is alive. God is stirring their hearts.

The more I worship in the new place, the more I appreciate the other. One is goosebumps and the other is mystery. One is the heart and the other is the head. One is new and the other is tradition. One is now and one is then. One the faith of my Father, the other the faith of my kids.

But both...together...are me.

They are both mine.

I claim them both and will forever because He led me to them. And I found Him there.

He is writing my story, and He wants to include it all.

I hope at the end of my life I can say I followed Jesus and He led me to every church to hear every song and pray every prayer. I want to say He led me to show me how alike we are and how much He lives in all of us even in our messiness. I think He is telling me to not put any limit on where He can go and what He can do.

Early on, He showed His face to me. He started a fire in my heart.

Now He is showing me how to keep my beautiful, faithful, seeking, burning heart open.

Wherever I am.

* What is your experience of church?

* How has your faith been supported by the community?

* What has changed for you about church throughout your life?

Grace Abounds

And this is the testimony of John, when the Jews sent priests and Levites from Jerusalem to ask him, "Who are you?"

He confessed, and did not deny, but confessed, "I am not the Christ."

And they asked him, "What then? Are you Elijah?" He said, "I am not." "Are you the Prophet?" And he answered, "No."

So they said to him, "Who are you? We need to give an answer to those who sent us. What do you say about yourself?"

He said, "I am the voice of one crying out in the wilderness, 'Make straight the way of the Lord,' as the prophet Isaiah said."—John 1:19-23 ESV

Every time I've read this passage before it has been about John preparing the way for Jesus. John wasn't the point of the story to me. Jesus was. And, of course, He still is. But today, for some reason, I was really feeling John.

They kept asking him, "Who are you?"

It made me think of how we ask people that all the time. Maybe not out loud so blatantly, but we try to figure out who people are so we can put them in a box. We ask others about them, we gather information based on outward signs, we judge, we condemn, we categorize, we google. We look them up on social media. We want to know, *Who are you?* But mostly, we want to glean a little more information about who *we* are by deciding definitively who *they* are.

We want to make people the hero or the villain because it makes us feel better. But the truth is no one person is only one thing. We can't define people by one moment in time or one bad decision or even years of making bad decisions. We are all works in progress. Human and in need of grace.

We rob ourselves of real communion with others when we place people in a box or on a pedestal. It's not right to outright dismiss or idolize mere human beings, but we do it all the time.

I've watched this play out in public on social media over the last few years, and it's tragic. People getting canceled, words getting twisted, assumptions being made, lies being shared, outrage and offense the order of the day. The name-calling if you don't agree, the shaming if you ask a question, the dismissal of anything that doesn't fit the crowd's way of thinking. This is not new.

John was leading people to Jesus. The people who didn't want to believe in the Messiah looked to discredit John. He didn't fit their narrative. He didn't line-up with their expectations.

Do you try to discredit people you don't understand? Do you jump to conclusions about others?

If someone wanted to know who you are, what would they hear from others? How would you define yourself? How do you describe others? Do you lead with a generous spirit?

Who are you?

* Who have you idolized or put on a pedestal?
* When have you been unfairly judged?
* Write about a time you unfairly judged another person.

Rocky Mountain High

It happened again this year.

As we were wrapping up our annual trip to Colorado and we were driving out of Steamboat, the sun was amazing over the mountains and the ground was blanketed in fresh powder, but I was crying. Tears were streaming down my face as we started our trek back home.

It's so holy in the mountains.

It just feels right, you know?

I love the line in "Rocky Mountain High" where John Denver sings, "Talk to God and listen to His casual reply..." His casual reply...those beautiful snow-capped peaks...the trees...the air. The clear night sky filled with stars scattered like promises. The magnificence and the simplicity. It's soul food. Every year I go there, and I fill up on nourishment for my soul. And when I leave, I fear it's not enough.

This year when I felt those tears and that familiar knot in my stomach as we drove away, I prayed. I talked to God. I told Him that I come to the mountains to find Him and He never disappoints but the thought of returning home to all of my "stuff" and my obligations and the cold and the flat lands and the monotony of it all scares me. I poured out my heart. And I listened for God's casual reply, and this is what I heard.

You come to meet me in the mountains because I'm so obvious there. It's good to have love and strength and power and might in your face like that. It assures you that I'm real and present and eternal.

My presence is undeniable in the majesty of the mountains and the trees and this beautiful land. I'm glad you like it. I'm glad it feeds you. I led you here to know that "soul rest" is possible and necessary.

But now I lead you home. I'm there too, you know.

I'm in the strong winds that blow across the desolate farmlands. I'm in the drifting snow.

I'm in your home. I'm in every nook and cranny. I'm in your kitchen with you every day, and I'm outside your window no matter the weather. I'm with you when you tuck in the kids and when you lay in bed reading your book.

I'm with you when you walk the dog and when you shovel the driveway.

I'm in the person next to you at the dry cleaners and the one in the car across the street. I'm in the grocery store parking lot, amid all the brown slush that has accumulated from all of the ice and snow and salt and traffic. It's not always pretty, but I'm there.

I can do beauty. I can do breathtaking views. But I'll go to the valley, and I'll trudge through the muck and I'll stay steady and present in the monotony of the day-to-day because that's where life happens.

Don't forget Me.

Don't make an annual trip the only time you feel My presence.

I am everywhere.

Create a home in Me, and You will never be alone.

* Where do you feel God's presence most profoundly?
* Describe a mountain top moment in your life.
* What is holy about where you live?

Prepare the Way

In church this week, the reading was about John the Baptist. The priest was talking about prophets. He told us everyone is a prophet.

That's right. Me and you. Prophets.

Do you believe it?

If not, change your mind today. Think of yourself as divinely inspired (you are) and filled with light (you are) and able to make a difference in the lives of people around you (you can).

He didn't call on the most learned, scholarly people to share the good news. He doesn't call people because they look perfect or act perfect or know everything. That wild man in the desert pointed to the Great Light. Don't you think He can use a suburban mom or dad or a high school student or a teenager who feels lost? Why wouldn't He use a CEO or a teacher or a doctor or a coach? Don't you believe He can use you?

What do you hear Him saying to you?

How is your heart feeling tugged?

What do you know to be true about God and faith and Jesus and the Good News?

Share it.

You are not disqualified. Don't believe the lie that you don't have enough education. Don't believe the lie that you don't fit the mold of what a prophet looks like. There is no mold. Jesus took all of that and threw it out the window. He plucked people out of the margins and encouraged them to lead. He will use you if You let him.

Let Him.

The world needs your unique voice. Even if it shakes. Especially when it shakes.

You know in your heart when He is calling you. You know the answer has always been and will always be, "Yes, Lord, use me." Say these words today. Don't hesitate any longer.

Use your voice to lift up the Lord. Be like John the Baptist and prepare the way.

Show people the light.

* How have you used your voice to honor God?
* How has God used others to speak life into you?
* What are you afraid of that is getting in the way of you sharing your faith?

That's in the Bible?

There are so many articles out there about "Ten Things You Need to Do to Be Happy," or "Five Steps to Fulfillment." Our social media feeds are filled with advice and instructions. Many of these points are things we all understand just from being human and living through some tough times. These lists are not groundbreaking, but they are good reminders.

I've created a list based on some of the advice we see from different writers, therapists, and coaches. I realized that all these points are also mentioned in the Bible, my go-to source of instruction. My how-to-do-this-thing-called-life book. It's all there.

No wonder I nod my head in understanding and want to share with others...this is Truth.

Where do you turn for the truth? How do you know if something is really true or if it's more of an opinion based on feeling? What is your source for truth?

Someone told me once that B-I-B-L-E stands for Basic Instructions Before Leaving Earth. I like that, but I feel like that makes it sound like we have to read it and follow it and then we might "get it right" before we die. It's not just something to figure out at a later date or something to follow so we get to heaven. God's Word is about *now*. It's about making *today* better.

We all live in communities. We have neighbors and schools and jobs and families. We have to learn to live together, hopefully in peace and harmony. It's not always a perfect Utopia but there are ways to build better relationships. It always starts with our own behavior. What choices can I make personally that will help me be a blessing in my communities? How can I live aligned with God's truth so that I can be a strong presence in my community?

Here's a list of some common instructions spouted out by writers and influencers and all manner of people on the internet, along with the corresponding verse in the Bible. What's really cool is most of these topics are mentioned *many times* in the Bible. All the things we are struggling with are not new. They are just tough. That's why we need so many reminders.

1. Give up caring what other people think of you.

> "For am I now seeking the approval of man, or of God? Or am I trying to please man? If I were still trying to please man, I would not be a servant of Christ."
> (Galatians 1:10 ESV)

2. Give up trying to please everyone.

> "You let the world, which doesn't know the first thing about living, tell you how to live."
> (Ephesians 2:2 MSG)

> "And you were dead in the trespasses and sins in which you once walked, following the course of this world, following the prince of the power of the air, the spirit that is now at work in the sons of disobedience."
> (Ephesians 2:1-2 ESV)

3. Give up participating in gossip.

> "Let no corrupting talk come out of your mouths, but only such as is good for building up, as fits the occasion, that it may give grace to those who hear."
> (Ephesians 4:29 ESV)

4. Quit worrying.

> "'Peace I leave with you; my peace I give you. I do not give to you as the world gives. Do not let your hearts be troubled and do not be afraid.'" (John 14:27 ESV)

5. Let go of insecurity.

> "'Therefore I tell you, do not be anxious about your life, what you will eat or what you will drink, nor about your body, what you will put on. Is not life more than food, and the body more than clothing? Look at the birds of the air: they neither sow nor reap nor gather into barns, and yet your heavenly Father feeds them. Are you not of more value than they?'"
> (Matthew 6:25-34 ESV)

6. Stop taking everything personally. It's not all about you.

> Do nothing out of selfish ambition or vain conceit. Rather, in humility value others above yourselves.
> (Philippians 2:3 NIV)

7. Give up the past.

> "Therefore, if anyone is in Christ, the new creation has come: The old has gone, the new is here!"
> (2 Corinthians 5:17 NIV)

8. Give up spending money on what you don't need in an effort to buy happiness.

> "But those who desire to be rich fall into temptation, into a snare, into many senseless and harmful desires that plunge people into ruin and destruction. For the love of money is a root of all kinds of evils. It is through this craving that some have wandered away from the faith and pierced themselves with many pangs." (1 Timothy 6:9, 10 ESV)

9. Give up anger.

> "Know this, my beloved brothers: let every person be quick to hear, slow to speak, slow to anger; for the anger of man does not produce the righteousness of God."
>
> (James 1:19, 20 ESV)

10. Give up control.

> "Many are the plans in the mind of a man, but it is the purpose of the Lord that will stand."
>
> (Proverbs 19:21 ESV)

So there you have it. Truth with a capital T.

* Write your own list of ten pieces of advice.
* What Bible verse do you think of most?
* Where do you go for truth and direction?

Community

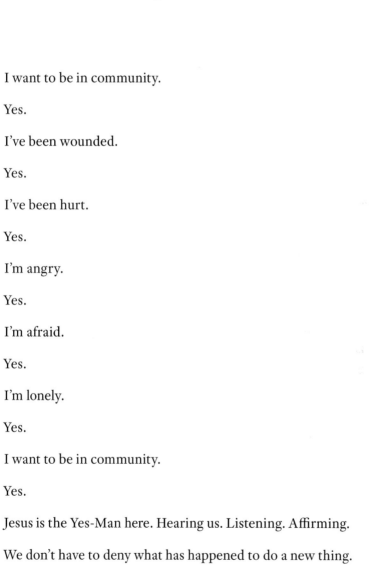

I want to be in community.

Yes.

I've been wounded.

Yes.

I've been hurt.

Yes.

I'm angry.

Yes.

I'm afraid.

Yes.

I'm lonely.

Yes.

I want to be in community.

Yes.

Jesus is the Yes-Man here. Hearing us. Listening. Affirming.

We don't have to deny what has happened to do a new thing.

We don't have to change what we want because we haven't gotten it yet.

We can bring it all to Him and lay it down at His feet.

Hurts and wounds and fear. Every part of us.

He won't even flinch.

He will listen. And He will hear. And He will affirm.

He will gently lead us to yes.

And then, anything is possible.

* What do you need to share with Jesus?
* How have you been hurt?
* What would you like to ask Jesus to heal?

Are You an Usher or a Bouncer?

Are you an usher or a bouncer?

I love this. Especially as it applies to Christians and church and community. To me this question is critical.

Which is it? Are you an usher or a bouncer?

Do you welcome people in, invite them to sit, shake hands, maybe hug, smile, accept, and connect?

Or do you shut people out, condemn, judge, deny, disconnect, and hurt?

What are we called to do as Christians? As humans?

I'm thinking of that song, "Rockstar" by Nickelback. *"I'm through with standing in lines to clubs I'll never get in..."* Can you hear it? Aren't we all? Who wants to not get in?

I love to read about Studio 54 and its heyday. I love music, fashion, and celebrities. I'm reminded now of the velvet rope and the bouncers and all the "pretty people" getting in while others waited for hours to be rejected.

Rejection hurts. Feeling *not enough* is the worst feeling—not pretty enough or rich enough or smart enough or good enough. We've all felt this way at one time or another and it hurts.

Author Karen Armstrong, said this: "Look into your own heart, discover what it is that gives you pain, and then refuse, under any circumstance whatsoever, to inflict that pain on anybody else."

Rejection gives me pain. I never want to make anyone feel rejected.

I want to be an usher.

An usher lightens the load for others. They say, "Welcome, come in, sit down, we've saved a spot for you, we were waiting for you, you are important, we are glad you are here."

This is how we build community. This is how we honor Jesus and His message. He said, "'Come to me all who are weary and burdened, and I will give you rest'" (Matthew 11:28). He didn't mention anything about the proper outfit or the right partner or the fancy background or the perfect past.

He invites everyone and when they show up in our lives, no matter where we are, we can usher them in. If not physically into a place, we can usher them into a feeling of acceptance and love with a smile, a connection, a helping hand. We can *see* them. We can welcome them.

With regards to the church, unfortunately, I have known a lot of bouncers. It makes me sad to think of this because so many people have been turned away from Jesus because of the bouncers at church living under a false notion that they are in charge of who gets in and out. It's sad and it's maddening and frightening and infuriating and pathetic really.

We are called to be ushers.

I am so grateful for all the ushers in my life. The ones who really know Jesus and His message of love. The ones who told me and showed me that to live in Christ is to live in joy. They welcomed me and showed me a path to generosity and kindness and wholeness and love and freedom.

We are all invited. Jesus is saving a place for *all of us* at His table. I don't just mean His table in heaven but also His "table" here on Earth. It's good to know when we get to the table—no matter the path we took to get there and no matter the shape we are in when we finally accept His invitation, and we show up—He will be there with open arms to usher us in.

* Who has welcomed you in?

* When have you felt rejected?

* How can you welcome others?

The Prodigal Son

I want to talk about the Gospel reading about the prodigal son (Luke 15:11-32). This is one of my favorites. It's the one about the father that has two sons, and he splits up the inheritance and gives it to them. One son stays with his father, works, and follows the rules. The other son leaves and squanders his wealth in wild living.

The lost son eventually spends all of his money and comes crawling back to the father. The father "caught sight of him and was filled with compassion. He ran to his son, embraced him and kissed him." He ended up throwing a huge party in his son's honor. The other son, the "good" son, was mad! He couldn't believe that the father would celebrate this person who lost everything when he had been so good!

The Parable of the Lost Son

Jesus continued: "There was a man who had two sons. The younger one said to his father, 'Father, give me my share of the estate.' So he divided his property between them.

"Not long after that, the younger son got together all he had, set off for a distant country and there squandered his wealth in wild living. After he had spent everything, there was a severe famine in that whole country, and he began to be in need. So he went and hired himself out to a citizen of that country, who sent him to his fields to feed pigs. He longed to fill his stomach with the pods that the pigs were eating, but no one gave him anything.

"When he came to his senses, he said, 'How many of my father's hired servants have food to spare, and here I am starving to death! I will set out and go back to my father and say to him: Father, I have sinned against heaven and against you. I am no longer worthy to be called your son; make me like one of your hired servants.' So he got up and went to his father.

"But while he was still a long way off, his father saw him and was filled with compassion for him; he ran to his son, threw his arms around him and kissed him.

"The son said to him, 'Father, I have sinned against heaven and against you. I am no longer worthy to be called your son.'

"But the father said to his servants, 'Quick! Bring the best robe and put it on him. Put a ring on his finger and sandals on his feet. Bring the fattened calf and kill it. Let's have a feast and celebrate. For this son of mine was dead and is alive again; he was lost and is found.' So they began to celebrate.

"Meanwhile, the older son was in the field. When he came near the house, he heard music and dancing. So he called one of the servants and asked him what was going on. 'Your brother has come,' he replied, 'and your father has killed the fattened calf because he has him back safe and sound.'

"The older brother became angry and refused to go in. So his father went out and pleaded with him. But he answered his father, 'Look! All these years I've been slaving for you and never disobeyed your orders. Yet you never gave me even a young goat so I could celebrate with my friends. But when this son of yours who has squandered your property with prostitutes comes home, you kill the fattened calf for him!'

"'My son,' the father said, 'you are always with me, and everything I have is yours. But we had to celebrate and be glad, because this brother of yours was dead and is alive again; he was lost and is found.'"

(Luke 15:11-32 NIV)

There is so much richness to this story. There are many layers of human emotion and sin and forgiveness and pride and humility and love and compassion. But I want to focus on the way the father greeted that lost son.

As someone pointed out to me once, the father didn't happen to see the son a long way off by coincidence. The father had been *waiting* since the son left. He had been waiting every day for his son to return! He was watching and hoping and praying!

I have been every character in this story. I have been lost; I have been found. I have waited, I have welcomed someone home. I have been mad and confused and indignant like the brother. I have been welcomed home. Haven't we all? Each time you read or hear the story, you see something different based on where you are in your life.

Here's the good news: we can go home anytime. We can return to God, and He will not turn us away. He is not like the older brother who demands retribution or punishment. He has been waiting for us. He is so happy to see us when we come home! I can imagine the son that had been lost thinking about how his dad would react to seeing him again. He was probably scared he would be punished or turned away. But instead, there was a party thrown in his honor!

I take this to mean no matter what I've done, no matter where I've been, no matter how long I've been gone, there is a place for me at the table. I have a heavenly Father who is waiting for me. He's waiting for you too.

If you haven't been home to God in a while, don't be afraid. He's waiting with open arms. He's ready to say these words: "We must rejoice, your brother who was lost has been found."

Welcome home!

* When have you been lost?
* Who in your life has welcomed you home?
* Who have you been in this story?

Silence

Do you ever pray for a sign and get nothing?

Do you ever feel like your prayers are met with silence?

I was listening to a wise pastor talk about silence. He said that God isn't silent because He doesn't have anything to say; He's silent because He already said it.

Often, you know the answer, you know the response to your prayer, you don't need more words. You just need to listen to what He has already said, what you know in your heart, what the Holy Spirit is telling you. But the world is loud, and we can only hear God in the silence, so we miss His voice.

He just wants to be with you. He knows you and you know Him, and together you can *just be*.

I remember learning and coming to know as truth the adage, "You know someone is a true friend when you can be comfortable with them in silence."

When you know someone well, you don't have to chatter incessantly. Although I will note here, I chatter incessantly with my best friend. It's like a stream of consciousness spoken out loud. We just laugh about how often we interrupt each other. As in, "Enough about you, let's talk about me!" One time, we had been shopping all day, and then we got back to her house and sat in her car and talked for hours.

Her husband came out to check on us. He walked out slowly, taking each step with care, like he was not sure what he would find. He asked her later, "What in the world do you have to talk about for that long?"

Even if we are talkers, true friends can be comfortable in silence.

I feel closer to God in the mountains. I think it's because of the silence. When you get high up in the mountains, it's silent. What's weird, though, is the silence has a sound. To me, it's the sound of acceptance. It's the sound of peace. It's like a huge exhale. It's as if God is saying, "Here it is; what do you think?" He created this magnificence, and, in the silence, we are reverent and awe- stricken at its beauty. We are left speechless.

In our world, we can be afraid of silence. We fill it up with words, talking incessantly, trying to make sure no one feels uncomfortable. We get in the way.

This happens a lot at funerals or when someone is grieving. We try to make them feel better by being chatty. We end up saying things that sound trite when just our silent presence would be more comforting. There is such a thing as the Ministry of Presence. Just be there and be quiet. Let God whisper words of comfort. Be a witness.

There's a song I chose to be "my song" on a retreat once. It's called "Testify to Love." One of the lines in it really stayed with me: "I'll be a witness in the silences when words are not enough."

Sometimes words are not enough. Sometimes silence is the best answer.

* When has God met you in the silence?
* Who can you be comfortable with in silence?
* When are words not enough?

The Balcony

I like going to different churches. I think it's fun to see the different ways Believers worship. God and His people are so creative. I'm a big believer that it's all holy, and if we open our eyes and hearts, we will see God everywhere.

My mom told me a story about her mother, my grandma. My grandma was beautiful. I mean exquisite. She was what you would call "lovely." She held herself with grace and dignity. She was intelligent and musical and spoke different languages. My mom claims she was "ahead of her time."

The story is that one time my grandma went to visit a different church because she wanted to hear the music. She didn't have the same music at her church, and she wanted to experience a different form of prayer and worship. She really loved it. She was in the front row of the balcony, and she was singing and dancing and waving her arms with the crowd. She was moved by the Spirit and was completely in the moment. She was having a great time—maybe a little too great—and she accidentally flung herself over the balcony! My mom told me this story years ago, and now it feels like maybe it was exaggerated a bit. After all, she's like me and loves a good story. I mean, how high up was it? Why were there no broken bones? But gosh I love the image. Knowing that no one was hurt, it really makes me smile.

When my mom and I were talking about it, we were hysterically laughing. How rare is it that we let ourselves be completely engrossed in the experience? Picturing her at that church with her hands in the air, singing and praising and dancing is such a beautiful image.

She tried something different. She wanted to experience God in a different way. She was not there to watch or judge or measure. She was there to participate. She was alive.

I'm not saying we have to fling ourselves over any balconies to prove that we are spiritual, but doesn't the dancing and singing sound fun?

How are you participating?

* What's your favorite way to worship?
* Describe a time you sought out a new experience.
* When have you been lost in the moment?

Hands

Have you ever looked at your hands?

I mean *really* looked at them?

I was listening to a priest who was explaining what happens when priests are ordained. He said that when they are ordained, their hands are anointed with holy oil. Their hands are anointed in anticipation of all the work they will be called to do. They will literally be Jesus' hands here on earth.

They will distribute Holy Communion and give blessings and perform baptisms and confirmations and weddings and funerals. They will lay their hands on others to signify forgiveness and reconciliation and healing. They will work for the poor and help the homeless and visit the imprisoned. They will greet and congratulate and anoint others. They will be busy.

Our hands are busy too. They hold babies and cook dinners and greet friends. They feel for fevers and fold laundry and sign permission slips. They tuck in and clean and organize. They type and they write and they "dial" phone numbers. They look up information and help with homework and they hold books. They zip zippers and tie shoes and pack lunches. They wave hello and goodbye and pat backs. They dry tears. They build with Legos, and they draw with crayons. They lift up in excitement and praise.

Some of our hands administer medicine and deliver babies and take vital signs. Some of our hands broker deals and sign contracts and write paychecks. Some of our hands help others walk or speak or learn. Depending on our jobs, our hands have different duties. Within a lifetime, our hands could do all these things.

People who cannot speak use their hands to communicate. Lots of people, like me, wave their hands around a lot when they talk in order to make their point!

When we're just getting to know someone and falling in love, holding hands is a big deal. To hold hands with someone is intimate and trusting and a way to say, "I like being with you."

My dad used to hold my hand when we walked. I haven't thought of that in a while, but now as I'm remembering, I can feel his hands. It was comforting to hold his hand. We were showing up together, as in, "I'm with him and I'm proud of it!"

In our former church, we would hold hands when we say the "Our Father," signifying we are one voice and one community in our prayer. I remember when this started. The first time I remember holding hands for "Our Father" was in college. It was a campus church, so it wasn't as traditional as my home church. My dad came with me once and gave me the side-eye when it was hand-holding time. He may have been thinking, "What is this hippy-dippy stuff?" But he didn't say anything; he just held my hand and prayed.

When someone is sick, we sit by their bedside, and we hold their hand.

Our hands show love and commitment. They say hello and goodbye and welcome. They work and they serve. They can transform, they can bless, they can pray, they can unite.

Yes, the hands of a priest are busy doing holy work. And so are yours and mine.

* How would you describe the work of your hands?
* In what ways do you feel called to serve?
* Where are you tight-fisted? How might you open your palms to receive what God has for you?

SHARING GRACE

Lord, thank you. For every moment, every person, every season. It all matters.

Thank you for the gift of language and writing. Help us to use it to draw closer to You.

Thank you for the gift of faith; help us find ways to share it.

Give us appreciation for and confidence in our original design. Thank you for the way You made us. Your creativity is seen through our uniqueness.

Show us how to embrace who we are so we can share our lives and our faith from a place of authenticity. Take away our fear as we step out to share grace with the people You have put in our path. Fill us up with Your grace Lord, so we can pour it out.

All for Your glory. Amen.

Putting on God's Armor

I was on the battlefield.

Actually, it started when they called me in for some more tests. The doctors saw something on the mammogram that was suspicious.

Of course, they didn't say this. They said that I need to come in for a bilateral screening and an ultrasound. Then they called back and said they take credit cards and asked if I wanted to pay right then over the phone.

Talk about adding insult to injury. No information. You might have cancer. You need to pay us.

Rude.

But since I was raised to be polite, there was a lot of, "Yes, ma'am" (actually that has nothing to do with my upbringing. I learned that when I moved to Texas at 45 years old). "Okay, thank you," and the one I say more often than I'd like to admit, "I'll be using my Visa..."

Then it started—the gearing up for the worst.

I know that there are a lot of false positives, and many women go in for extra screening and they don't find anything. I just read an article about the different opinions among doctors about how often screening is needed and the concern that maybe all this testing is causing undue stress.

But none of that matters when it's you.

I also know people that have cancer, people that have beat cancer, and unfortunately, I know others who have lost their battles with this awful disease. It's a formidable foe. It's scary.

I was so cognizant of my every move and thought that day. I was hyper-aware in the hospital, taking it all in as if it was my last time I'd see these things as a healthy person. I felt like I was in the "before" scene… "before she knew." There were signs, literature, smiling faces. There was a "wishing you the best" from the registration lady. Some people lowered their eyes. There was seriousness. There was a prayer box.

I'm lucky. It turns out there is "nothing to worry about."

But now, I'm just not buying that. I will worry about it. Not every day but some days. I'll worry when I hear a friend has to go in for another test. I'll worry when I do. I'll worry when I hear the news that a friend has cancer. I worry the phone is going to ring with bad news. I'll worry about my kids and my friends and my husband and my friends' kids and I'll worry about myself. Not every day but some days. Not all day but for some of the day. I'll forget and things will be going along and then I'll remember.

This is what I mean when I say I was on the battlefield.

As a Christian, I believe the battlefield is in between my ears. It's my mind. It's the worry, overthinking, analyzing, predicting, anxiety, regret, and insecurity. It's my mind that tells me not to trust.

So I went there yesterday. I went into my mind. I faced it head-on. I took my heart and my trust and my faith and my Savior that walks with me. I took them all into the battlefield of my mind. As I was lying on the examining table for the ultrasound, I just prayed. I prayed that God would be with me and I felt Him. I prayed that I could handle whatever news came my way and I felt a release. I prayed that I would walk this path with grace and humility and acceptance, whatever comes. And I felt a keen sense of grace, humility, and acceptance.

God says to *ask*. Ask...Seek...Knock. Don't just lie down on the battlefield and give up. Don't let your mind talk you out of your faith. Don't forget Him.

> "Finally, be strong in the Lord and in his mighty power. Put on the full armor of God, so that you can take your stand against the devil's schemes. Stand firm then, with the belt of truth buckled around your waist, with the breastplate of righteousness in place, and with your feet fitted with the readiness that comes from the gospel of peace. In addition to all this, take up the shield of faith, with which you can extinguish all the flaming arrows of the evil one. Take the helmet of salvation and the sword of the Spirit, which is the word of God. And pray in the Spirit on all occasions with all kinds of prayers and requests. With this in mind, be alert and always keep on praying for all the Lord's people."
>
> (Ephesians 6:10-11, 14-18 NIV)

They say there are no atheists in foxholes. I believe it. There are probably no atheists in cancer wards either.

After all, we cannot go into the battlefield alone. Thank God we don't have to.

* In what ways have you struggled with your health?
* What do you do when you feel fearful and worried?
* What has God taught you in times of uncertainty?

Rainbows

I don't know how many times I've set out to "read the whole Bible." In order. Now I know this is futile. Honestly, most people start strong and get to Leviticus and quit. My advice now is to start with John.

But this is a story of a time when I was still gung-ho and freshly enthusiastic to start with Genesis.

After reading Genesis, I was thinking about the one word that popped out for me and it was "covenant." A covenant is an agreement or a contract between two parties. A promise, but weightier.

Right after I was finished with my first few days of reading and I had written "covenant" in the margin of my schedule for Bible reading, I received a photo from my friend who is in Chile. It's a photo of a rainbow. The symbol of God's covenant with us! Is this a coincidence that He sent this to me on this day? No, of course not. This covenant business is real. And God is so creative and fun, isn't He?

He shows us signs all the time.

He showed me signs of His love when He sat me next to a woman who said she started praying when her child was sick, and then "her whole life just became a prayer." How awesome is that? I mean, her *whole life became a prayer.*

He showed signs of His love when He blessed a ministry I started with a friend, called Flourish, with amazing women with open hearts and the willingness to be authentic and vulnerable. He's in those hugs and laughs and "me too's." He is in every brave woman who takes that next step even when it hurts and it's hard and she's not sure where she is going.

He showed me signs of His love when a friend reached out to encourage me, when she said, "I understand" and "I believe in you" and "I'm proud of you." He's in that friend's generosity of spirit and giving heart.

He's in the sun that breaks through the clouds on a cold winter day just to remind us, "This too shall pass."

He's in the phone ringing at just the right time and the hand reaching out before the fall and the kindness of strangers.

My friend was working for a ministry that provides meals and shelter for homeless men and women. They also help with job interviews and resumes and getting people back to work so they can be self-sufficient. One day I was getting ready to give some of my husband's old work clothes to charity, so I asked my friend if she needed any suits and business clothing for men. She called me back the next day asking, "Is there any chance you have anything in a size such and such?" And I looked and there it was...all the clothes I had were the perfect size for a man that was heading back to work the next week. He needed clothes and we had the perfect size. Coincidence? I think not. As my friend said, "This is how God works."

These miracles are happening all around us, every day. God is fulfilling His promises and carrying out His plan in big and small ways. He is faithful.

Once you realize this, life becomes an exciting adventure of "What miracles will happen today?"

Keep your eyes open. You don't want to miss the rainbows.

* What does covenant mean to you?
* Where have you seen God working in your own life?
* What miracles have happened to you today?

God's Promises

In Bible study today, we made a list of our worries. Then we thought of God and His promises and wrote a truth from God's Word over each worry.

God will provide.

God will protect.

God will finish the good work He started.

God loves us.

God forgives.

God heals.

God gives us strength.

God gave us a spirit of power and self-control.

God is mighty.

God is sovereign.

God tells us not to fear.

God gives us peace.

God gives us clarity.

God will lead us.

I could go on for days. For every worry, there is a truth that we know from God's Word that will ease our hearts and minds.

Make a list. Keep it close to you. Better yet, memorize it. Write it on the tablet of your heart.

* Who is God? What do I know to be true about Him?

* In what ways does God's Word bring peace to my heart?

* Write a letter to God. Let Him know what you are worried about and ask Him to help you find peace.

If You Were a Tree...

"It's my birthday, and I'll .... if I want to."

See the blank? I get to fill it today. I know the song says "cry," but I don't feel like crying. With all the caffeine I had this morning, I feel like flying. Actually, that would be awesome, except I'm a scaredy cat.

My husband went skydiving once and loved it. He was all jacked up on adrenaline. I was happy for him, but it's not for me.

My friend asked me today if I was excited it was my birthday. It reminded me of something.

When I turned six, I memorized a poem by A.A. Milne. Here it is and here's me at six!

"When I was one, I had just begun.

When I was two, I was nearly new.

When I was three, I was hardly me.

When I was four, I was not much more.

When I was five, I was just alive.

But now I am six. I'm clever as clever.

I think I'll stay six now forever and ever."

I used to run around reciting that one. Obviously, I did not stay six forever and ever. And I haven't used the word clever since then.

So, in honor of today, I'd like to offer some new thoughts.

Our life's work is like building a tree. (Stick with me here, I'm working up to something.)

Childhood is the trunk of the tree. It takes years to build a steady, solid base. The trunk has nicks and cuts on it. It is bruised and worn in parts, but it is strong. "That which doesn't kill us makes us stronger" makes sense. These are the years we build our character.

Young adulthood is where we build the branches. Each one juts out in a different direction based on what we choose. The branches represent school, dating, marriage, children, career, friendships, faith, and passions. Each individual tree is shaped differently based on our lives. Please note, in this young adult area, we may build some branches that need to be pruned later. Just sayin...

When we are in our forties and fifties, we add the leaves. We beautify the tree. We add leaves and flowering buds with our works of charity, loving, volunteering, parenting, guidance, accomplishments, listening, understanding, and wisdom. Again, some branches may remain empty depending on our mood when someone asks us to volunteer. I can just picture it now—my beautiful tree. On the branch that says PTA, it's void of any life, not even a bud.

This is the stage where we accept that our tree does not look the same as everyone else's and we embrace it. We may even try to stand apart by adding a swing or a hammock. We may get really crazy and offer ourselves up for a treehouse! We laugh more, accept more, embrace more. We get comfortable.

When we are in our sixties and above, we enjoy the tree. We will continue to add to the tree, but by now, we have a beautiful, joyful, nurturing, protecting, and loving tree. We are content to sit in the shade it provides or lie on the hammock it holds or swing on its swing. We have built something real, something solid, and something sacred.

If we are lucky and God grants us the gift of more birthdays, we can enjoy the tree for many years. We can continue pruning (getting rid of the rotten buds like anger or resentment or regret) and taking care of it (with love and gratitude) so we can leave something beautiful and life-giving for future generations.

So, back to the question...am I excited about another birthday? Heck yes! I'm getting closer to the part where I lie in the hammock.

Life is good.

* How would you describe the tree of your life?
* What in your life needs to be pruned?
* What are some things you love about the season you are in now?

Live Your Story

"Occasionally weep deeply over the life you hoped
would be. Grieve the losses. Then wash your face.
Trust God. And embrace the life you have."

—John Piper

Life isn't perfect. It's not always easy. But honestly, it's all we've
got. This one life we are living.

We spend a lot of time reading and watching other people's stories.
But ultimately, it's our story we want.

When we are in the midst of something hard, we think, "I wish
my story was different." But in hindsight we see that it couldn't
have been.

There is no "better life" or "better story." It's not like that. You
are designed to live *your* story. What is making you miserable is
all the wishing that it was different.

What if *today* you got curious about your story?

Explore:

How has God protected me?

How has God provided for me?

What is God preparing me for?

Write about your joys.

Write about the people you love.

Write about your gifts and talents.

Ask God to show you some of the highlights.

Ask God to walk with you through the plot twists and the extra characters.

Open your eyes to what is unfolding.

Acknowledge what has been built.

Commit to running *your race.*

Start *living* your beautiful story.

It's the only one you've got. And ultimately, it's the only one you want.

> "Tell me, what is it you plan to do with your one wild and precious life?" —Mary Oliver

* What does it mean to embrace the life you have?
* Ask God to show you how your story is part of His story. Write about it.
* What are you excited about?

Jesus Wept

You know the story of Lazarus. Jesus was friends with Lazarus and His sisters, Mary and Martha. The sisters came to Jesus and told Him that Lazarus was very sick. Jesus waited a couple of days to go see Lazarus. Lazarus was dead. Jesus wept along with the sisters and friends who had come to mourn. Then He called to Lazarus and brought him back to life. He did this so people would believe. We were talking about it the other day in Bible study and while there is so much more to it, these two words stand out.

Jesus wept.

We think, why? Why didn't He just fix it? Why didn't He just make everything how He wanted it? Why didn't He just save His friend?

We do the same thing to Him in our lives. We think, *Jesus, just fix it. Do it now. I know you can. I don't want to suffer.*

Who actually *wants* to suffer?

But suffering is part of it.

There is no glory without suffering. We get to share in His glory and it will be magnificent, but first, we have to live our lives. And living in this world includes suffering.

There was another school shooting in the news this week. It's heartbreaking. And maddening. Why can't we prevent this?

What do we need to do to make sure this doesn't happen again? We cry out to God, *Fix it, God, fix it! Take the evil out of our world. Take away pain and death.*

We get mad and we start yelling. In our anger and frustration, we lash out. It's so awful we implore someone to make it stop. God? Congress? The President? Doctors? Law enforcement? Judges? Schools? Churches? Neighborhoods? Parents? Curriculum? Social media? We demand answers and accountability.

We wonder where God is.

But then we see Him. He is with the families of the victims, and He is weeping. He is with the parents picking up their kids who are safe, and He is weeping. He is with the family of the shooter, and He is weeping. He is with us as we watch the news, and He is weeping.

He hasn't left us. He is the God of hope and peace and new life. There will be time for that.

First, He weeps.

* When in your life have you felt God grieving with you?

* Write about a time when your personal suffering brought you into a closer relationship with Jesus.

* Think about what makes you weep and bring it before the Lord in prayer.

It Won't Keep You Safe

It won't keep you safe.

Going to church. Eating dinner as a family every night. Reading to your kids before bed.

All the books about parenting, all the Sunday school classes, all the family vacations, and "perfect" Christmas mornings that you work so hard to pull off. They are not a guarantee.

I used to think if I did all the "right" things, then my kids would be healthy and happy and successful. I thought if they were healthy and happy and successful, then I would be too. So, I gave myself an assignment.

Do it all. Do it right. Guarantee your future and the future of your children.

Buy a house in the best neighborhood, get in a good school district, show up for everything at school. Volunteer, join groups, get to know the other moms. Be involved in the community. Go to church. Serve at church. Go to Bible study. Work out every day. Be healthy. Be polite. Cultivate a strong marriage. Read books. What am I forgetting?

There were always debates about working moms vs. stay-at-home moms. It doesn't even matter.

There were debates about private school vs. public school. It doesn't even matter.

There were debates about everything. Breastfeeding vs. formula. Store-bought baby food or homemade baby food. Lots of activities or more time at home. And then the ultimate debate... college. I saw two grown men go to blows over which college is better, University of Illinois or University of Michigan? I mean, really? A fist-fight. The pressure on these kids to get into the college of their parents' choice...gross. Knowing what we know now, there is an argument to be made that college is not worth the price. It's definitely not for everyone. But even if our child may thrive *not* going to college, is that something we are willing to consider? What if it doesn't fit our expectations?

So much of our time is spent when we are younger trying to control everything.

So much of our time is spent when we are older realizing how we have control over nothing.

They are who they are. They will do what they will do. They are on their own journey. Let them live.

What if you actually *don't know* what is best for them?

Advice for my younger self: Love them for who they are. Spend all your love loving them, not trying to fix them or control them.

I mean, think about it. God actually *can* control our lives. But He allows us to be free.

We *cannot* control their lives, but we keep them on a short leash.

God lets us be free because He is secure in who He is. He has no need to make us His showpieces. He doesn't need us to validate His worthiness. So, He loves and offers guidance, but we get to choose to mess it all up if we want. And when we do, He still loves and offers guidance. It's not a personal affront or an attack on who He is as Father.

I want to be like that.

I have not always been like that.

This realization has caused me deep pain. I wish I could go back. But what would I do differently? Honestly, nothing. And would it change anything? Lord knows, I don't want to do the junior high years over again. I'm so tired.

Moms, I know you fought hard. I know you sacrificed. I know you cheered and baked and bought and showed up and went to the doctors and therapists and OT and speech teachers and PT and music lessons. I know you deliberated and worried and cried and laughed and celebrated. You waited for diagnosis and advocated for proper treatment. You gathered at IEP meetings and asked for help. You said yes to a lot of stuff you didn't want to do. You arranged and rearranged and made calls like it was your one job in life.

And still, maybe it didn't turn out like you planned. Or at least, at this moment, you can't see the fruits.

God tells me that while things may not always look the way I envisioned, all of the time and energy and love I gave to my kids does count. It does matter. They will return to it. They will remember the kindness, the attention, the laughter. Lord, please help them remember the laughter.

They will leave and come back. They will fail and get up again. They will take you for granted and then call one day oozing gratitude. They will misread you and judge you and complain about you. And then they will call you in need because you are the one they can trust, and they know it. You will feel like they don't appreciate you. You may feel like you've lost them. You will be scared, you will worry, you will wonder, *What did I do wrong?*

Take it to God.

He understands parents because He has to do it too. He has lived through the 3 a.m. calls, the tears, the begging, the pleading, and the hopelessness. He has waited patiently for His kids to see the light. It's a process, He assures me.

I think He is talking about my kids. I make it about them getting their acts together while God and I lovingly wait. I assume He is reassuring me that they will see the light, that I should be patient. But He is not talking about them at all. He is referring to me.

Stubborn. Self-centered. Lost. Placing value on the world's prizes.

He's waiting. Patiently. Arms open. Forgiving. Stable. Unafraid.

What a beautiful example.

Lord, help me be more like You.

* How have your own children taught you about you?
* What is God showing you through your parenting?
* How can we be more like God the Father?

Losing at Checkers as a Kid

I grew up with two older brothers. They always beat me at games. And being the youngest and only girl, I would get frustrated and throw the game board and stomp away. Any of you remember doing that when you were younger?

We don't do that as adults. Thank God. But we feel like it sometimes, don't we?

Or maybe you have done that. Not getting the answer you wanted, maybe you lashed out. Not getting results quickly enough, maybe you quit.

Maybe you made a scene, sought revenge, or severed relationships because things weren't going your way.

But now maybe you wished you would've waited, that calmer heads would have prevailed, that you would have chosen to trust God's plan.

There's no failing, only learning. So what have you learned?

I've learned that God is for me. And He loves me enough to prune away my immature and selfish impulses. I've learned that what I feel in a moment is fleeting. I've learned that good, solid things take time.

I've learned that pride comes before the fall.

And faith and trust are the building blocks of everything I long for.

It's a marathon, not a sprint. If you are feeling frustrated or alone or misunderstood or ripped off, wait. Be still. Pray. Trust.

God is doing something beautiful. It may feel like a mess now, but He brings beauty from ashes.

All you have to do is get out of the way. Stay at the table. Take a loss if that's what you need to do. Handle it with humility and grace.

Do not throw the board and stomp away. You've come too far for that. This is so much bigger than that one game.

* How have you learned to handle anger or disappointment?
* What do you regret?
* How do you feel about competition?

Legacy

Sometimes I wonder what my legacy will be.

There is so much talk in the news, on social media, and in books about *finding purpose* and *living a life of meaning*, I think we can get overwhelmed wondering, *Do I matter?*

We can list off our accomplishments and maybe that feels good. It's good to have goals and meet them. But is that legacy?

We can look at our bank account and the assets we have and that might feel good. But is that legacy?

While one definition of legacy is "the amount of property or money left to someone in a will," that's not the one I'm referring to.

I like this definition: "the long-lasting impact of particular events, actions, etc. that took place in a person's life."

Long-lasting impact.

Think about the people in your life whose words or actions have had a *long-lasting impact* on you.

I venture to guess these people were not celebrities. Their influence probably didn't come from a movie set or a microphone on a stage. I'm willing to bet it wasn't an Instagram or Tik Tok influencer who had a long-lasting impact on your life.

It's probably someone you know personally.

So when we say we want to leave a legacy, do we mean a long-lasting impact on someone's life? If so, we can start today with the people in front of us.

Or do we mean that we want to be famous, well known, popular, and rich? Because that's fleeting and temporary, not legacy at all.

I think of my mom and dad, always there for me, trustworthy, kind, faithful, and loving. Their words and actions live for generations through their kids and grandkids.

I think of my husband, standing beside me all these years, holding on through the ups and downs, steady, solid, funny, and loyal.

I remember the Believers who have shared God's truth with me. Sometimes it felt like a slap and other times a hug, but it stuck, and it changed me for good. They stood on a firm foundation and invited me to stand on the rock with them.

I think back to the times when I sat in rooms with people who were vulnerable and honest, who told their stories and who listened to mine with acceptance. They taught me that shallow is safe and boring, and I am called to go deep.

I think of the friend who said, "That's not who you are," just the reminder I needed at the right moment because she had taken the time to really know me and love me. The friend who forgave me. The friend who rooted for me, for my kids, for my marriage. The ones who prayed for me. They taught me that we are better together.

I think of my kids, growing and changing and learning. Showing me I don't know everything but also reminding me that I do know a lot. They show me my flaws and they solidify my strengths. Because of them, I recognize my capacity to love is much larger than I ever knew.

I think a lot of people think of their kids when they think of their legacy. I hope my kids know they are loved beyond a shadow of a doubt, by God first and by us too. My hope and prayer is that my kids know they can always call us. We are always here. No matter what is happening, good or bad, reach out to us. We will never leave. We belong to each other. We are here to stay.

All of these people who have impacted my life long-term have something in common. They taught me to stay. They taught me *by staying*. They anchored down, said yes, committed, and followed through. They are still here. Maybe not right here, next to me in Texas, but they are with me forever. In my mind and in my heart and in my memories. Their legacy is strong.

So when I think about my legacy, I hope to emulate them. I started this book with an essay about my mom and dad and God, all stayers. All rooted. Sure-footed. So coming to the end it makes sense that I'm still talking about that.

Oh, I know there are things that are shinier and more exciting than staying. I know bright, shiny objects can draw your attention. And that can be fun for a time. Enjoy this life. But remember what you really want. I mean, when you look back on your life and think about your legacy.

Think about what you will leave behind. Choose what you want that to be and then start building your days with it as your guiding light.

Be the most important kind of influencer.

* What does legacy mean to you?
* Write about someone who has impacted your life long-term.
* What do you want *your* legacy to be?

What Now?

I'm at that part of life that people call, "The Second Half." Carl Jung first popularized the phrase, the "two halves of life."

"The first half of life is devoted to forming a healthy ego, the second half is going inward and letting go of it."
— Carl Jung

The practice of journaling helps us go inward.

When I look back at my story and the notes I've been keeping through journals, I see all the stages I have gone through. I see God's Hand guiding me as I move through them. Now, I'm in midlife, and I'm an empty nester so everything is changing.

I'm taking on a new role in this new season. Sometimes I don't even know what that role is.

There is grief and loss, as well as excitement and relief.

I can see why people wonder if the best years are behind them once they reach their fifties, but I have to believe there is so much more good to come. I look forward with joyful anticipation. Maybe this is just optimistic Sue, wearing rose-colored glasses. The girl who was raised to look on the bright side, be grateful, and smile!

But then I remember, God always has more for me. If we are breathing, He has something for us.

Recently, I had a doctor's visit that brought about more questions than answers. I had been through this before. It turns out

I'm okay, so this is not about my health as much as it is about God's provision.

It was interesting because my doctor's visit was on Ash Wednesday. My doctor had ashes on her forehead, reminding me of my Catholic background. This had to mean something, right?

When they give the ashes, they say, "From dust you came and to dust you will return." Sounds kind of morbid but honestly, it's refreshing.

We are here for just a bit. A blip on a screen. A moment in time.

I think of all the years, standing in line to receive ashes. But now I don't.

Why would God have me go to the doctor with ashes on her head at the beginning of the Lenten season?

Because He loves me.

He calms my fears with the familiar. The divine thread is there. From birth to now, He has not left. He will not leave.

The ashes are a sign to rest, to enter into a season of doing less, to spend time with God. The ashes remind me that our lives are made up of seasons. I've been through so many. The ashes are also the reminder of His redemptive story.

A time of sacrifice leads to a time of joyous celebration.

Tough seasons end and we smile again.

We share in Christ's suffering, and we share in His glory.

The crucifixion leads to the resurrection.

There is always hope.

Good Friday is dark but there will be glorious light on Easter morning.

Some days are awful and soul-wrenching, but God.

Maybe this is the gift. Looking back and recognizing His hand in everything.

I don't know what is coming next.

But I do know God has me.

And I know the ending.

It's magnificent. More beautiful than we can imagine.

His promises are true.

No matter what comes, my answer to God will always be, "Yes, Lord, Yes, Yes, Great Big Yes!"

* How does God remind you of His presence?
* When have you been in a spiritual wilderness?
* How will you face the future with joyful expectation?

This is not the end of the story. God has so much more for you and for me. He continues to write a beautiful story. What an honor to be a part of it! I can't wait to see what He does next.

There will be love and loss and laughter. There will be mystery and agony and victory.

His grace will be with us through all of it.

Expect miracles.

Carry a pen.

Write it all down.

The best is yet to come.

Keep saying, "YES!"

About the Author

Sue Bidstrup is the founder of Great Big YES Coaching and Community. She is a Life Coach who focuses on helping women begin and sustain a journaling practice. She has worn several hats over the years, including hosting a podcast, creating and facilitating an online coaching group for entrepreneurs, speaking to women's groups, teaching Christian yoga and serving in many different ministries.

She has been writing in her journals since middle school and started her blog, Great Big YES, in 2010. Sue currently leads an online journaling community for women. Sue has used journaling as a tool for herself and her clients, finding it to be extremely helpful for mental, emotional and spiritual clarity and peace. She loves helping women learn more about themselves and God through the practice of writing.

Sue is a natural-born cheerleader, and encouraging others is a big part of her original design. She has an enthusiasm that is contagious and a relatability that draws others to her. She is approachable and meets others where they are without judgment. She leads with her heart, sharing with vulnerability, and invites others to do the same.

Sue and her husband, Jeff, have been married for 29 years. They have three grown children who are out of the house now, so they spend their time fawning over their dog, Gus. They lived in the Chicago area their entire lives until a job change for Jeff moved the family to Austin, Texas, almost ten years ago. They immediately bought a truck, started their cowboy boot collection and secured tickets to Austin City Limits (the TV Show). When she's not reading or writing, you'll find Sue out and about, drinking coffee, listening to live music and enjoying the sunshine.

You can follow Sue on social media @greatbigyes and at greatbigyes.com.

Made in the USA
Monee, IL
01 September 2023

41980004R00152